Blame it on Beckett

by John Morogiello

A SAMUEL FRENCH ACTING EDITION

FOUNDED 1830

SAMUELFRENCH.COM

MUSIC USE NOTE

Licensees are solely responsible for obtaining formal written permission from copyright owners to use copyrighted music in the performance of this play and are strongly cautioned to do so. If no such permission is obtained by the licensee, then the licensee must use only original music that the licensee owns and controls. Licensees are solely responsible and liable for all music clearances and shall indemnify the copyright owners of the play and their licensing agent, Samuel French, Inc., against any costs, expenses, losses and liabilities arising from the use of music by licensees.

IMPORTANT BILLING AND CREDIT REQUIREMENTS

All producers of *BLAME IT ON BECKETT* *must* give credit to the Author of the Play in all programs distributed in connection with performances of the Play, and in all instances in which the title of the Play appears for the purposes of advertising, publicizing or otherwise exploiting the Play and/ or a production. The name of the Author *must* appear on a separate line on which no other name appears, immediately following the title and *must* appear in size of type not less than fifty percent of the size of the title type.

In addition the following credit *must* be given in all programs and publicity information distributed in association with this piece:

BLAME IT ON BECKETT received its world premiere on October 16, 2011 at Abingdon Theatre Company (Jan Buttram, Artistic Director; Kim T. Sharp, Associate Artistic Director; Samuel J. Bellinger, Managing Director) in New York City, NY

BLAME IT ON BECKETT was produced by the Abingdon Theatre Company in New York City on October 16, 2011. The performance was directed by Jackob G. Hofmann, with sets by Andrew Lu, costumes by Kimberly Matela, lighting by Duane Pagano, and sound by David Margolin Lawson. The Production Stage Manager was Mark Hoffner. The cast was as follows:

JIM FOLEY	Warren Kelly
HEIDI BISHOP	Lori Gardner
TINA FIKE	Anne Newhall
MIKE BRASCHI	Mark Doherty

CHARACTERS

JIM FOLEY - 40, a dramaturg.

HEIDI BISHOP - 25, an intern in the literary department.

MIKE BRASCHI - 35, the general manager of the theater.

TINA FIKE - 63, a famous playwright.

ACT ONE

(In the darkness, we hear the voices of a panel discussion at a theatre conference.)

MODERATOR. And lastly, we have distinguished Beckett scholar, Dr. E. L. Whisty.

(light applause)

WHISTY. *(British accent)* Good evening.

MODERATOR. Dr. Whisty, what do we mean when we speak of Beckett?

WHISTY. No, no. I'm afraid I must disagree with your question right out of the gate. To speak of Beckett is to speak of everything and nothing in the cosmos in one simultaneous death rattle of peripatetic stasis.

*(Their voices begin to fade. **JIM** enters in the darkness and takes his place at the desk.)*

MODERATOR. I don't understand.

WHISTY. Exactly.

MODERATOR. Could you clarify what you mean?

WHISTY. No.

(Light applause is heard. The sound fades as the lights come up on the literary office of a regional theater in New England. There are faded posters of past productions on the back wall. One poster, tilted, is for a play called Woman Of The Corn *by Tina Fike. The wall itself is composed of unpainted cinder blocks. The entrance to the room is a heavy steel door with a vertical, chicken-wired window just above the knob. Upstage right of the room heading off stage is another door with a handwritten sign taped to it. The sign reads "Conference." The room itself contains a number of chairs and two old,*

7

metal desks completely covered with play scripts, ashtrays, old coffee cups, and yellow legal pads. There is a small shelf of old books, upon which sits a blindfolded bust of Shakespeare. Upon Jim's desk is a laughably old computer, a phone, and a beat up desk lamp.)

Scene 1

(At rise: JIM, overwhelmed, sits at his desk talking on the phone. His sports jacket is draped over a far chair, which is also covered with scripts.)

JIM. Don't be silly, I love talking to you. I love talking to all our playwrights.

(JIM grabs a coffee cup. Disappointed to discover it is empty, he throws it in the trash.)

...Well, my assistant's out. You should see my desk; they're piled up to the ceiling. –I'm sure I did...Let me find it...

(JIM crosses to his jacket. He pulls a pack of cigarettes from his pocket, puts one in his mouth. He feels his pocket for a lighter.)

What was the title again? ...What do you know? Here it is, right on my desk...Have I read it?

(JIM crosses back to the desk, looking for a lighter.)

No. But the reader lov...well, I can't read everything. Not everything's worth reading. ...Of course, *yours* is worth reading! See, the *reader*–the reader thought it was fabulous.

(Over the following, HEIDI enters quietly, with a large shoulder bag. She is eager to make a good impression. Seeing JIM on the phone, she gestures an inquiry whether or not she should leave. JIM casually gestures that the call is unimportant.)

JIM. ...I'm reading it off the page right now:

(JIM crosses back to the chair and tilts it, dropping the scripts to the floor.)

Fab-U-Lous.

(JIM taps the chair. HEIDI sits, putting her bag on the floor beside her.)

JIM. ...No, I can't read you the entire report. That would violate our reader confidentiality policy...Hang on a sec.

(JIM *covers the phone and speaks sotto voce to* HEIDI.)

Lighter?

HEIDI. What?

JIM. Matches? Anything?

(HEIDI *shrugs an apologetic negative.* JIM *returns to the phone, crossing to the desk.*)

Listen, my twelve o'clock is here. I would love to answer your questions. (JIM *tries to light his cigarette against the desk lamp bulb.*) Love it. Love it. Love it. But I can't. ...Tomorrow? Perfect. Same time. (JIM *gives up, turning off the desk lamp.*) ...I'll read it tonight. Okay? You're talented. We love you. You're wonderful. You're fabulous. Keep sending us scripts. Bye-bye. (JIM *hangs up the phone and drops his cigarette.*) Oh GOD! What an asshole!

HEIDI. Who was it?

JIM. Just another neurotic playwright. He's calling same time tomorrow. Remind me to be in conference.

(JIM *picks up another empty coffee cup. He throws it in the trash, knocking a cup of pencils off the desk.*)

HEIDI. *(picking up pencils)* Are you Jim?

(JIM *crosses to a coffee cup atop scripts upstage left.*)

JIM. Mm hmm. Heidi?

(JIM *shakes the cup. It is empty. He crosses right and tosses it in the trash. Done with the pencils,* HEIDI *stands. She grabs a coffee cup downstage right and shakes it. She tosses it in the trash.*)

HEIDI. Should I–? Do you have to read his play now?

JIM. I'd be lucky to *find* it. This is just the "in" pile.

(HEIDI *grabs, shakes, and tosses another coffee cup.*)

There are three times as many scripts at my house, insulating the walls.

(**HEIDI** *finds a coffee cup by the conference room door, which is ajar.*)

HEIDI. How are you going to read it by tomorrow?

JIM. I won't. I'll be in conference.

(**JIM** *gestures to the conference room.* **HEIDI** *peers into it.*)

HEIDI. Why is there a bed in the conference room?

JIM. Does it make you nervous?

HEIDI. Depends on your definition of conference.

(**HEIDI** *closes the conference room door.* **JIM** *feigns innocence.*)

JIM. A nap. What did you *think* I meant?

(**JIM** *crosses to desk.* **HEIDI** *crosses in.*)

HEIDI. The theater lets you nap–?

JIM. *(warning)* Ap!

HEIDI. –*conference* whenever you like?

JIM. The theater lets actors nap.

(**HEIDI** *tosses her empty cups in the trash.*)

I just usurp it.

(**JIM** *tosses a cup from the desk into the trash.*)

Shows with a large cast sometimes have to dress in here.

(*The phone rings.*)

HEIDI. Should I go?

JIM. Don't be silly.

(**JIM** *takes the phone off the cradle a half inch and puts it back down. The ringing stops.*)

HEIDI. Oh, um–

JIM. You wanted a meeting, right?

HEIDI. Yeah, but I don't want you to–

(*The phone rings.* **JIM** *takes it and replaces it again.*)

Could you stop–? That makes me uncomfortable.

JIM. More than the bed?

HEIDI. I'll come back.

> *(**HEIDI** crosses to her bag.)*

JIM. Come back, the phone will still be ringing. It's always ringing.

> *(The phone rings. Lift, replace.)*

HEIDI. *(putting bag on shoulder)* Don't you have voicemail?

JIM. If it's full, the calls come through.

> *(**HEIDI** starts to exit. She stops and turns to **JIM**.)*

HEIDI. You should check your messages.

JIM. I'd like to, but the phone keeps ringing.

HEIDI. Can't the receptionist hold your calls?

JIM. Suddenly I'm a CEO.

> *(**JIM** dials the receptionist. He speaks as if the receptionist is his best friend and he is about to tell her that the captain of the football team is in love with her.)*

Hi Angela. Jim. Any calls? ...Really? The phone must be on the blink again. ...Could you hold my calls for awhile? I'm in a meeting with Mary Poppins. ...You *know* I love messages. Take as many as your little hand can scribble.

> *(**JIM** hangs up.)*

Better?

> *(**HEIDI** puts her bag beside the chair again. **JIM** discovers a butane lighter under a script. He tries repeatedly to ignite it.)*

HEIDI. You're not supposed to smoke in the building.

JIM. Really. That's very interesting.

> *(After a few more attempts, **JIM** gives up lighting the cigarette. He slaps both lighter and cigarette on the desk.)*

Start talking.

HEIDI. About?

JIM. About why you're here. About what you want from me this early in the week.

(**HEIDI** *begins tidying the fallen scripts on the floor.*)

HEIDI. I'm looking for a job.

JIM. Have you tried the McDonald's?

HEIDI. *(a trace of annoyance)* A job in the theater. Well, I kind of already have one, just not in my specialty.

JIM. Any theater job is a great place to start–

HEIDI. I work in the box office.

JIM. –except the box office.

(**HEIDI** *stares at* **JIM.** *She puts the scripts atop the pile beneath the tilted poster.*)

HEIDI. ...Is there anyone else I can talk to? Joseph Tilson?

(**HEIDI** *straightens the poster.*)

JIM. Joey's directing in New York.

HEIDI. Maybe I should wait 'til he gets back.

(crossing downstage left)

Janet suggested that I talk to him.

JIM. Ah, but you see, he's never back.

HEIDI. He's the literary manager.

JIM. Nominally. He comes in once a month for half a day and doesn't talk to anyone. Joey is the big-name bait that lures the unsuspecting playwright fishes onto the hook of our submission process.

HEIDI. Who are you?

JIM. I'm the dramaturg; the guy who reels them in, clubs them, and throws them back for being too small. I run this place. It all comes down to me.

(**JIM** *opens a desk drawer. Inside is a cup. It has a little coffee left.*)

Finally!

(He takes a sip as his watch alarm beeps. **JIM** *turns off the alarm. Over the following,* **JIM** *pulls four prescription pill bottles out of his desk. He takes a pill from each, one at a time, followed by a swig of coffee.* **HEIDI** *crosses to him.*)

HEIDI. I know what a dramaturg is.

JIM. That's half the job right there.

HEIDI. I just got my MFA in it.

JIM. God, you're completely unemployable. So, box office girl, are we selling out?

HEIDI. It's only my third day. I'm here to be a dramaturg.

JIM. I'd love to make you an offer. Love it, love it, love it. I just lost my assistant to the miracle of motherhood. Don't tell anyone, but she's taking the maternity pay and quitting.

HEIDI. I could be your assistant.

JIM. But I can't hire you. Our big thirtieth anniversary fundraiser turned out to be a fundlowerer. Big Mike Braschi controls the money. So I'm afraid– *(He has run out of coffee, but has one pill left in his mouth.)* Anything in that cup?

(JIM gestures downstage right. HEIDI crosses to it and picks it up.)

HEIDI. This one?

(JIM nods.)

Half an inch.

(JIM waves her over.)

It's really old.

JIM. So was the other one.

(JIM downs the last pill with the coffee.)

So, I'm afraid Janet set you on the wrong path.

HEIDI. She suggested I read.

JIM. *That* I can offer. Please. Grab a script.

HEIDI. Any script?

(JIM gestures to the pile downstage right. HEIDI, with slight hesitation, takes one.)

JIM. You can take more than one, if you like.

HEIDI. Can I?

(JIM *slaps all of the pill bottles back into the desk and slams the drawer closed in one fluid motion. He throws his arms in the air.*)

JIM. Take them all!

HEIDI. I'll start with one.

JIM. Read it. Write a report. Some time next week we'll get together and you can tell me what's in your report so I don't have to read that either.

HEIDI. *(crossing to desk)* How long should it be?

JIM. No more than a page, synopsis, analysis, recommendation, that sort of thing.

HEIDI. Recommendation?

JIM. Is it a keeper or a crapper.

(HEIDI *sits in the chair and starts to put the script in her bag. She is stopped by* JIM*'s line.*)

HEIDI. I don't want to discourage their creativity.

JIM. By next week you will. Bad playwrights should be discouraged at every opportunity. *This* is what comes of encouraging bad playwrights.

(JIM *stands and crosses down left of* HEIDI)

Three thousand different scripts every year. Did you know that there were three thousand people writing plays in this country? *(crossing to the downstage right pile of scripts)* And each of them had a high school teacher or a professor or a friend encouraging them to "write what they know." *(grabbing a script from the pile)* What have we here? "I, Polyphemus: A Character Study." I thought a character study was something the playwright did *before* he wrote the play. Now, it turns out, it's the play itself. What would Aristotle think?

HEIDI. I doubt Aristotle would get the opportunity to see it.

JIM. *(crossing up right of the desk)* But you're wrong. This excrescence comes with a production history. A reading in Virginia. A festival production in D.C.– has anyone ever truly enjoyed a festival production

JIM. *(cont.)* anywhere? Now imagine one in Washington, D.C.! This is the sort of play small, urban theaters drool over; contemporary, small cast, no set, maybe the occasional gay character.

HEIDI. Polyphemus is contemporary?

JIM. It's an updating of the Cyclops legend set in an alley of inner-city America. They talk. You get to know them. And one blinds the other to show us the randomness and horror of it all. Why? We don't know. That's what makes it modern.

(**JIM** *tosses the script in the trash.*)

HEIDI. What type of play are you looking for?

JIM. *(crossing downstage right)* I am on safari for the perfect dramatic structure. The great white structure hunter. Don't give me issues. Don't give me experimental. Give me a strong dramatic base.

HEIDI. Is that it?

JIM. Is that it??? I'm asking the impossible. There are only a handful of plays dating back to Aeschylus with perfect dramatic structures. *(crossing downstage left)* They're the reason we're here. The ones that touched us in such a way that we have dedicated our lives to finding or helping to create others like them. Where every character has a purpose. Where everything introduced gets brought back. Where every scene ends with a reversal that propels you on to the next. And it's all so logical and perfect and delicate, that all you can do when it is over is wonder…and marvel…and sigh, because you know that it will never be as beautiful as this again.

(**JIM** *directs this at* **HEIDI** *as he walks back to the desk.*)

Like a new lover, the play has revealed all of its secrets to you.

HEIDI. Wow.

JIM. But don't bother looking for it here. This office is where great theater goes to die. *(sitting on the edge of the desk)* There hasn't been a truly great dramatic writer since Shaw.

HEIDI. What about Beckett?

JIM. He's the one I blame for all this mess. *Waiting for Godot* wreaked more havoc on Western drama than Oliver Cromwell. *(crossing to upstage left pile of scripts)* Every grad student who ever read *Godot* immediately dismissed Beckett by saying, "Well, I can do *that.*" And then they'd toss off some horrible, derivative tract. Plot was pronounced dead. Killed off by a playwright nobody likes.

HEIDI. I like Beckett.

JIM. No you don't. Nobody does.

HEIDI. I do.

JIM. You're too young to like Beckett. You just say you like him because you've been told he's a genius. Your professors said:

(JIM grabs a script and stands atop a smaller section of the pile.)

"This is good," and like the dutiful little academic lemming that you are, you jumped off the French/Irish cliff.

(JIM steps down.)

HEIDI. *(after a sigh)* –You probably want to know what script I took.

JIM. God, no.

HEIDI. *Requiem For a Hairdresser.*

JIM. Oh! Patrick Donnelly's play!

HEIDI. *(putting the script in her bag)* How'd you know that?

(JIM sits at the desk, grabbing a pencil and a post it pad.)

JIM. He was the guy on the phone. –Let me log you as the reader. …Heidi Bishop, Hairdresser. Could be your business card!

(He writes down the information and immediately crumples the paper and throws it away.)

HEIDI. You can't scare me.

(**HEIDI** *stands and crosses downstage right.* **JIM** *puts his feet on the desk.*)

JIM. The last thing I want to do is strike fear in the hearts of the box office staff.

HEIDI. I see. You can't frighten me, so you try to insult me.

JIM. They didn't teach you about occupational ennui in your little dramaturgy school?

HEIDI. So it's the degree that threatens you?

JIM. The only thing that threatens me is that sweater.

HEIDI. Look, I'm no deer before the headlights. I just spent a shitload of money on that degree and I intend to use it.

JIM. You spent it, or Daddy spent it?

HEIDI. *(crossing to the exit)* Leave Daddy out of it.

JIM. Oooh, paternal issues.

HEIDI. *(turning on him)* I have no paternal issues.

JIM. *(putting his feet down)* But he's a rich man who wouldn't pay for his daughter's college.

HEIDI. He's not rich.

JIM. Then why does his daughter wear Christian Louboutin? Shoes like that don't come from box office work, honey, they come from a daddy: Be he genetic or be he sugar.

HEIDI. Okay, Dad bought the shoes, but *I'm* the one–

JIM. Did he pay for your education?

HEIDI. What does this have to do with–?

JIM. It's my job, to find the drama. Who paid?

(**HEIDI** *steps closer to* **JIM.**)

HEIDI. Everything I earned, I earned myself. I fought my way through school and now I'm going to fight my way into a job.

(crossing down right)

Unlike you, apparently, I love theater. I love the idea of a single person in front of a blank page creating a global mythology for the masses. I want to help that person realize her full potential. I want to become a dramaturg.

JIM. We have no need for melodrama.

HEIDI. Fuck off.

JIM. *(elated)* Mamet we can use. Will I see you next week?

HEIDI. *(crossing)* You'll get my report tomorrow.

(**HEIDI** *stumbles over her expensive shoes as she exits.* **JIM** *laughs. The scene change audio begins as the lights fade.)*

Scene Change 1

(Applause and award show music, which fades quickly as the **WINNER** *begins speaking.)*

WINNER. *(voice over)* I'd like to thank the American Theatre Wing and my fellow nominees for this award–the cast, the director, all two hundred and eighty-seven producers. You know, I wrote the first draft over fifteen years ago after an immense personal loss and–

(The play off music begins, gradually getting louder. The **WINNER** *tries to talk over it, eventually rising to the pitch of hysteria.)*

–whoa, that was fast, um… –No one would touch it for the longest time! I think it was five years before I had the first reading! –But I kept plugging away!! Just the writing itself was cathartic!!! –IT HELPED MITIGATE THE NAGGING URGE I FELT TO COMMIT SUICIDE! –BUT I'M MUCH BETTER NOW, THANKS TO YOU!! –I DON'T FEEL WORTHLESS ANYMORE!!! …No, I'm not leaving; it's my stage. Do you know how long I–? FUCK YOU! FUCK ALL OF YOU!!!

(The play off music becomes loud enough to drown out the **WINNER**'s *screams, then fades.)*

Scene 2

(The next day, late afternoon. **JIM** *sits behind his desk, four pages into a yellow legal pad covered with inked notes through which he frequently flips. Occasionally,* **JIM** *refers to a copy of Tina's play on his desk.* **TINA**, *in dark, frumpy clothing, sits furthest from* **JIM**, *looking dour.* **MIKE**, *in stylish business attire–but no suit jacket– stands apart from them.)*

JIM. I see what you're saying.

TINA. I mean, I can make the change–

JIM. I think it would–

TINA. But Janet hasn't indicated–

JIM. *(overlapping)* I haven't mentioned it to Janet.

TINA. *(continuing)* –anything to me about that kind of change. You're talking about a major–

JIM. Not that major.

TINA. –overhaul. It's all of act two! I don't know if I'm willing–

JIM. Let's just think about it, okay? Two-five through…Two-ten. It's six pages, it's not an overhaul.

TINA. *(sitting on the back of her chair)* But it affects the rest of the act.

JIM. Six pages of monologue that have nothing to do with the plot.

TINA. But thematically it ties the whole thing together. Look at *Iceman.* Would you tell O'Neill to cut out Hickey's monologue?

JIM. You *know* I would. Right after I told him to cut out the Chivas.

*(*TINA *steps off the chair and lies on the floor.* **MIKE** *crosses to down right and leans his head against the wall.)*

We're moving on, okay? Just look at it. You don't have to do anything. You know that. You don't have to make any changes at all.

TINA. Don't patronize me.

JIM. *(rolling his chair toward* **TINA***)* All I'm saying is that if you're going to bring this into New York–

TINA. I thought we were moving on!

JIM. *(rolling back to the desk)* Okay: Act Two, page –fourteen? Fourteen…Sharon says…Where's my pen?

TINA. *(sitting up)* Where is that?

JIM. No. I can't find my pen. Third one I've lost today.

MIKE. It's on your ear.

*(***JIM*** *retrieves the pen from his ear.* **MIKE** *crosses upstage right.)*

JIM. Sharon: "A man's blood is thick, as thick as the wad of bills he carries. But a woman's blood is boiled by love, which will outlast all the money in the world." I'm not getting the metaphor.

TINA. What's not to get?

JIM. Everything. It makes no sense. You can do better there.

TINA. *(to* **MIKE***)* Did you understand the line?

JIM. What are you appealing to him for? He doesn't know.

TINA. *(standing)* Mike, were you getting it?

MIKE. Not really, but so what?

JIM. See? He's useless. Don't talk to him.

MIKE. *(smiling)* I'm not useless.

JIM. To me you are.

MIKE. I'm just not a dramaturg.

JIM. Turge.

MIKE. Whatever. The line doesn't matter. Cut it, leave it in; either way it won't affect ticket sales.

TINA. *(sighing)* I'll cut it.

*(***TINA*** *sits in the chair.)*

JIM. I win again. I do it because I love you, Dumpling. Your script needs to be as ready as possible before it's out of my grasp. If it goes to New York, you won't have me anymore.

TINA. I can bring one person from the originating theater.

MIKE. Yeah, but you're gonna want a business guy, not a dramaturge.

JIM. Turg.

TINA. I don't give a damn about that. If the script isn't ready Jim's coming with me.

JIM. And who's gonna do all this, with Renee gone? Joey??? I don't think so. Nuh-uh, I don't leave this office.

(**MIKE** *sits on the upstage right edge of the desk.*)

TINA. You'll come if I call. Everyone does.

MIKE. Maybe for this one, they'll let you bring two people.

TINA. Since when?

MIKE. I'll make a call.

(**HEIDI** *enters, carrying a covered cup of coffee and her bag.*)

HEIDI. Oh, I'm sorry, I–

JIM. Right with you.

HEIDI. Oh my God, you're Tina Fike. You're like the most amazing playwright who ever lived. You're up there with Shakespeare in my opinion.

TINA. *(to* **JIM***)* Just hand me the rest.

(**TINA** *stands and gathers her things.* **JIM** *tears the pages off the pad and hands them to* **TINA***.* **TINA** *walks past* **HEIDI** *abruptly.*)

I'm gonna miss my train.

JIM. Let me show you out. Be right back.

(**JIM** *follows* **TINA***.*)

HEIDI. I look forward to seeing your play.

(**TINA** *ignores* **HEIDI***.* **JIM** *shushes* **HEIDI** *and escorts* **TINA** *out.* **MIKE** *and* **HEIDI** *are left alone. She puts the coffee on the desk.* **MIKE** *smiles at her.*)

MIKE. She treats everyone like that.

HEIDI. I suppose she can afford to.

MIKE. Still doesn't make it polite.

HEIDI. I studied her plays in college. Even directed one for the drama group.

MIKE. Make any money?

HEIDI. We did it for free.

MIKE. Let's hope we get a little something out of this one. We need it.

Mike Braschi. General manager.

(**MIKE** *offers his hand.* **HEIDI** *shakes it.*)

HEIDI. I know you. I wave to you every day.

(**HEIDI** *sits in the chair.*)

MIKE. Do I wave back?

HEIDI. Of course you do, you're very friendly.

(**HEIDI** *takes* Requiem For A Hairdresser *from her bag.*)

MIKE. *(embarrassed)* …I'm…You work here?

HEIDI. Heidi Bishop. I'm in the box office.

(**MIKE** *stands and crosses upstage of the desk.*)

MIKE. Sure. Every time I walk through the lobby. I didn't recognize you without the plate glass. What are you doing in literary?

HEIDI. Reading scripts. Box office is just a job. This is where I'd rather be.

MIKE. Jim could use the help until Renee gets back.

HEIDI. I heard she isn't coming back.

MIKE. *(sitting in desk chair)* I've yet to hear anything.

HEIDI. Jim said yesterday–

MIKE. *(smiling)* I would need to hear it from Renee, wouldn't I? In order for me to act on it?

(**MIKE** *puts his feet up on the desk.* **HEIDI** *moves the coffee to the floor beside her chair.*)

I would need something in writing. I'm not going to pay two people for the same job.

HEIDI. Two people?

MIKE. I can read between ambition's lines. You're looking for Renee's job.

HEIDI. Are you offering?

MIKE. I can't. Are you asking?

HEIDI. Just…floating a proposal for future use.

MIKE. *(putting his feet down)* Get back to me after Tina's play opens. If it's a hit, maybe we can do something.

(MIKE stands and starts to exit.)

HEIDI. I'll hold you to that.

MIKE. *(facing her)* Hold me any way you want. It's money preventing it, that's all.

(MIKE turns to leave again. HEIDI stands, leaving the script on the desk.)

HEIDI. How about an internship?

MIKE. *(turning to her)* Meaning?

HEIDI. Meaning I do all the stuff Renee used to do, part time.

MIKE. Do I have to pay you?

HEIDI. No.

MIKE. You got it.

HEIDI. *(a quiet celebration)* Yes!

MIKE. You like Jim's work?

HEIDI. *(joking)* God, no. I like Jim's job.

MIKE. *(amused)* That's a good attitude.

HEIDI. I'd do so many things differently.

MIKE. *(crossing to HEIDI)* Like what?

(JIM enters between them and heads to the desk chair to sit.)

JIM. Back from the dramaturgical abyss.

MIKE. *(to HEIDI)* Excuse me.

(MIKE crosses right of the desk, to JIM.)

Can I ask you what that was?

(HEIDI sits on the upstage left pile of scripts.)

JIM. What.

> (**MIKE** *leans on the desk. His hand is on a pad.*)

MIKE. That stuff to Tina about not talking to me. You mind?

JIM. *(taking the pad, forcing* **MIKE** *to move)* I didn't want her getting an uninformed opinion.

MIKE. Meaning?

JIM. Well, you're not exactly the office wordsmith.

MIKE. Go on.

JIM. That's *my* job.

> (**MIKE** *crosses upstage right.*)

MIKE. *(smiling)* Then you stick to being the dramaturg–

JIM. Turge.

MIKE. *(turning back to* **JIM***)* Thank you. –And I'll concentrate on the business. Just make sure nothing lousy is on the page. I got a call this morning that we lost our operating grant. If we don't get Tina's play into New York, there's gonna be some big changes around here.

JIM. The script is fabulous. She just has to lose the monologue in act two.

MIKE. Whatever needs to happen, you to make it happen. Get that thing humming ahead of time. We need you here, not New York.

JIM. It would be easier, if I had an assistant.

MIKE. *(a quick glance at* **HEIDI***)* What about Renee?

JIM. Oh stop, you know all about Renee.

MIKE. She make that much difference?

JIM. My toilet backed up this morning, you know what I found there? A one-act verse drama about Tallulah Bankhead.

> (**MIKE** *crosses downstage right of desk.*)

MIKE. How about an intern?

JIM. Anything.

MIKE. *(to* **HEIDI***)* There you go.

(**MIKE** *exits*)

JIM. What was that??? I swear, the man is insane. Nobody likes him.

(**JIM** *puts the pad and Tina's script into his attache.*)

HEIDI. *(crossing down left and looking after **MIKE**)* Oh, I don't know…

JIM. That talk about the intern? It's just blah blah blah, blah blah blah blah. Is he going to get me one or not?

(**HEIDI** *turns to* **JIM**)

HEIDI. He already has.

JIM. …You?

HEIDI. *(sitting)* Part time.

JIM. *(standing)* Oooooh, who just made kissy-face with Big Mike Braschi?

(**JIM** *crosses left of Heidi's chair*)

HEIDI. I didn't make "kissy-face."

(**HEIDI** *picks up her script.* **JIM** *crosses upstage left.*)

JIM. Two minutes alone with him: "Oh, Mr. Braschi, you're *so* powerful! You can hire and fire whomever you like."

HEIDI. I did not.

JIM. "I sure would like to show my mean old Daddy I'm not a failure."

HEIDI. Cut it out.

JIM. *(crossing down left)* Take it from me, honey, that boy is not your type. No college degree for Big Mike Braschi.

HEIDI. So?

JIM. Don't say "so," it's too defensive. It stops the conversation. I close up and you get no more information. Say "Really?" So we can dish.

HEIDI. …Really?

JIM. *(moving to **HEIDI**)* I swear to God! Between us: Mike Braschi has only a GED.

HEIDI. How did he get to be General Manager?

JIM. *(making them sound horrible)* Hard work and ambition. Can you believe it? –He started out as an usher.

(JIM sits on the edge of the desk)

HEIDI. Why no college?

JIM. Something about his father. I don't pay attention to his little stories. Neither should you. *My* stories will be far more beneficial to your professional development.

(JIM sits in the desk chair. He shakes an empty cup to see if there's any coffee in it. He makes a face and throws the empty cup away.)

HEIDI. All I did was tell him how glad I was to work at a theater dedicated to new plays.

(JIM emits a screaming cackle. He quiets down.)

JIM. Sorry. You were serious.

(He adjusts the script and pad in his attache.)

HEIDI. A lot of great plays have come out of this theater.

JIM. Yes, but only one per annum. *(JIM's watch alarm beeps. He turns it off.)* Whoops. –First job for the intern. Fetch me some coffee.

HEIDI. *(handing him the cup from the floor)* Done.

JIM. You making kissy-face with *me* now?

HEIDI. God forbid.

(JIM pulls the pill bottles from his desk and lines them up. He opens the bottles and takes the pills over the following.)

JIM. One new play per season, that's our limit. You work in the box office, you know how the season is set up.

HEIDI. I know the ticket prices.

JIM. Almost every major non-profit is the same. We open with a classic comedy–kind of a season-opening celebration to tell people: "We're *fun!* Who cares if summer's over! Wasn't seventeenth century Paris a laugh riot?" Then we do our new play. Tina's. We've softened them up with the comedy, now we hit them with the unknown, to remind them that at some point we used to be artists. After that, we're coming on to the holidays, so we have three options: a Christmas play, a lavish musical, or a family classic. Usually we combine these precious choices by trotting out the reanimated corpse of Jacob Marley for the eighteen zillionth time.

(JIM *slides the pill bottles back into the drawer and closes it in one fluid motion.*)

After the holidays, in an effort to reach out to a traditionally non-theater-going demographic and to satisfy the criteria of most of our major grants, we proudly trumpet our "black play." *(standing and crossing downstage right with his coffee)*

The "black play," by the strangest of coincidences, always seems to occur during Black History Month, just when every other theater, museum, orchestra, and cultural institution has scheduled their "black events" too. So nobody comes, not the "black people" who have too many other places to go that month, and not the "white people" who refuse to spend their money on a "black play,"– *(crossing to* **HEIDI***)* –which is truly a shame because it is usually the only show of the whole season I actually enjoy. *(crossing down left)*

In March and April we have our "Irish play," to reassure the "white people" that we know they once had it tough too. *(crossing upstage left)*

Then we end the whole thing with a classic drama; a really popular one; with a big star; something that will touch them; something that will have each and every member of that audience leaving the theater shouting: "My God! I have never felt such a burning desire to resubscribe!" *This* is what you've gotten yourself into. Three thousand script submissions for one slot on the season. Our purpose is not the propagation of playwrights. Our purpose is to endure.

(JIM *sits in the desk chair.*)

HEIDI. I know I can't change everything right away–

JIM. What about your little job in the box office? What is that, minimum wage? How will you survive in an unpaid second job?

HEIDI. I won't need to for long. Renee's job will be all mine.

JIM. But if Signor Braschi can get you to do it for free, why should he hire you?

HEIDI. He wouldn't do that.

JIM. *(standing)* All right, then: welcome to the belly of the whale. *(crossing to the other desk)* Somewhere under all of that there used to be a desk.

(JIM *shoves the scripts on the floor, clearing a small space for her.)*

HEIDI. This is so cool.

(HEIDI *sits at the desk and removes an old book from her backpack. She inhales its fragrance and places it on her desk with something just shy of reverence.)*

JIM. What's that? *(reading) The Complete Plays of Hrosvitha of Gandersheim?*

HEIDI. Have you ever read it? She was, like, this medieval nun who wrote plays when most of the Western world was illiterate. Can you even fathom what this woman was trying to accomplish in a male society? And an anti-theater society! She wrote because she needed to. Read this part.

(HEIDI *opens the book to a page and hands it to* JIM, *who crosses downstage left as he reads.)*

JIM. "I did not dare lay bare my impulse and intention to any of the wise by asking for advice, lest I be forbidden to write because of my clownishness. So in complete secrecy, as it were furtively, I tried as best I might to produce a text of even the slightest use."

HEIDI. "To produce a text of even the slightest use." That's why we're here. Us, in this office.

JIM. They don't mention the translator.

HEIDI. *(crossing to* **JIM***)* It doesn't matter. It's just some cheap, knock-off textbook. But it was my bible in college. That and Tina's plays.

(**HEIDI** *takes the book and returns it to her desk.* **JIM** *sits at his desk.*)

JIM. Where shall we start?

HEIDI. *Requiem for a Hairdresser.*

JIM. *Requiem for a Hairdresser.* Did you do your report?

HEIDI. *(retrieving a page from the script)* Right here.

(**JIM** *grabs his legal pad and searches the desk drawers for a pen. He finds one.*)

JIM. Shoot.

HEIDI. If you read the report...

JIM. I don't read reports. I jot down insightful comments for the rejection letter.

HEIDI. What if I didn't reject it?

JIM. Then you didn't do your job.

HEIDI. Seriously.

JIM. Oh God, you didn't–

HEIDI. It's a good play.

JIM. Okay, you're new. I understand you want to be nice. Just don't.

HEIDI. Why do you stay in this job if you hate it so much?

JIM. I love the job. I just don't like bad plays. The literary management is a pain. Renee handled that, and now you will too. All this mess? That's yours. My energy goes into the dramaturgy, researching and working on a script in rehearsal with people like Tina Fike. That's the fun stuff.

HEIDI. Will I get to do any of that?

JIM. You can observe. Here. (**JIM** *hands* **HEIDI** *a script from a desk drawer.*) Tina's play. First preview's in two weeks.

HEIDI. Thanks.

JIM. Read it over, especially Act Two, page five. Tina's not being cooperative.

HEIDI. Then what?

JIM. We can talk about it. You can sit in on rehearsals and meetings if you want.

HEIDI. Awesome.

JIM. The only thing I ask in return…is that you change your report on *Requiem for a Hairdresser* to a rejection.

HEIDI. *(standing)* Read it.

JIM. I don't need to, I can tell it's bad from the binding.

HEIDI. It's not bad.

JIM. Of course it's bad; it's by Patrick Donnelly!

(**HEIDI** *puts Tina's script and another from the floor on her desk.*)

HEIDI. I'm taking this one too.

JIM. Don't ignore me. You think I need an intern that badly?

(**HEIDI**, *ignoring* **JIM**, *crosses to the phone and dials.*)

HEIDI. What are you going to do? Big Mike Braschi gave me the job.

JIM. Don't tell me you didn't make kissy-face!

HEIDI. *(into phone)* Hi Angela, Heidi Bishop from the box office… I'm going to be helping Jim Foley out in literary. Are you still taking messages from yesterday?

JIM. Don't do it.

HEIDI. I'll be right down to pick them up. You can forward us the calls again.

(**HEIDI** *hangs up.*)

JIM. Ooh, you little trollop!

(*The phone rings.*)

HEIDI. *(exiting)* That's for you.

JIM. *(yelling after* **HEIDI**, *then answering the phone)* You better come back bearing donuts. –Literary…Patrick Donnelly, right on schedule…If you hadn't, I was going to call you…Mm-hmm, last night and I loved it. *Loved* it…What do you want to know? …End of scene two? Could you hold on a second?

(*JIM reluctantly grabs Heidi's report from her desk as the lights fade and the scene change audio begins.*)

Scene Change 2

PROFESSOR. *(voice over, German accent)* All plays can be reduced to a single mathematical formula: Characters plus goals plus obstacles. Somebody wants something, but they can't have it.

Characters want things. They *need* things. That's what theater is–that's what LIFE is–in a nutshell: humanity's unquenchable longing for that which it cannot have. Characters plus goals plus obstacles. This formula works for all plays, all movies, all television shows. It works for Shakespeare. It works for Spongebob. Watch: Hamlet wants to avenge the murder of his father, but he cannot kill the king, his uncle, who's married to his mother. Plankton wants the crabby patty formula, but Mr. Crabs won't let him have it. You see?

American playwright and critic John Howard Lawson put it a little differently in his 1960 book, *Theory and Technique of Playwriting*. Lawson suggests that drama stems from a conflict between Conscious Will and Social Necessity. Vladimir and Estragon want to leave (that is conscious will), but they are prevented from doing so by the social necessity of their appointment with Godot. Plankton consciously directs his will toward the securing of the crabby patty formula, but Bikini Bottom society will not allow the theft of corporate secrets.

Naturally we could put John Howard Lawson's biography into a similar dramatic context: Lawson wanted to write plays, but the House Unamerican Activities Committee blacklisted communists.

(This one may be faded at any point, preferably after the second paragraph, based on how long it takes to clear the stage of the mountains of scripts and coffee cups.)

Scene 3

(A week later. Heidi's effect on the office is manifest. The desks are clear of scripts, cups and debris, though Jim's is a little less organized. Uncluttered, the office seems larger and colder than it was. As the lights come up, **HEIDI** *is sitting at the second desk–now hers–talking on the phone. She sprays a can of air freshener as she speaks. A script lies open on one of the chairs. A newspaper is open in front of her.)*

HEIDI. …The Lifestyles section…*Lifestyles,* the one with the obituaries. *(sharpening a pencil)* …See the picture? That's the woman I'm working with. Her play opens next week…I thought you'd be– *(standing)* Sure, I talk to her. "Hello. I like your work." …You know. Dad. I haven't the slightest interest in the starting salary of a chemical engineer. I gotta go.

*(***HEIDI*** hangs up quickly and angrily. She throws the newspaper in the trash. She crosses to her bag and pulls a few coins from her purse. She quickly counts them and shakes her head. Returning the coins, she sits, grabs a script, and takes a sip of coffee. The phone rings. ***HEIDI*** sighs and answers it.)*

Literary…Sure, which one is yours?

*(***HEIDI*** sits on the edge of the desk.)*

…Ah, we just sent it back. Yesterday. …The letter will tell you what we thought. –No, we don't do form letters anymore, we changed that policy. We're also taking e-submissions now, so if you've got something new– …Sure, what do you want to know? Let me get the report. Hold on.

*(***HEIDI*** puts the caller on hold and crosses toward the conference room when ***MIKE*** knocks quickly and enters. He carries a number of script sized envelopes.)*

Hey!

MIKE. Brought up your mail.

HEIDI. You didn't have to do that.

MIKE. Jim around?

HEIDI. Not yet.

MIKE. Any idea when?

HEIDI. He usually drags in about eleven.

MIKE. Does he?

HEIDI. -ish.

MIKE. I can come back.

HEIDI. I'll call down to let you know.

MIKE. Your phone's out.

HEIDI. Jim just says that when he doesn't want to take calls.

MIKE. *(Smiling. Stepping into the room.)* Really?

HEIDI. You never knew that?

MIKE. I suspected. I mean, I never called the phone company. I had nothing in writing.

HEIDI. Well, you don't have to worry about it anymore. The policy's changed.

(He puts the mail on one of the desks.)

MIKE. Looks like a lot of things have changed around here.

HEIDI. Not as much as I'd like.

MIKE. –Read anything good lately?

HEIDI. Not really. Bunch of sterile dramas about sensitive young playwrights being acted upon by a hostile universe.

MIKE. Who wants to see that?

HEIDI. Exactly. We need issues.

*(**MIKE** leans against the downstage right wall.)*

MIKE. Issues are a trap. People want relationships.

HEIDI. A play has to be about something.

MIKE. A family's not something?

HEIDI. Something important.

*(**MIKE** smiles.)*

You know what I mean. We're here to challenge an audience.

(**HEIDI** *moves to her desk.*)

MIKE. But you're not, that's the trap. All those guys that wrote "classic" American plays–they wrote domestic dramas. Then comes the nineteen sixties and theaters start dealing with "issues" to shake people up. *(crossing to the desk)* And they did it. They shook all the Republicans out of the audience. Only the liberals, who agree with the issue to begin with, attend the theater. Non-profit theater is just a way of making rich Democrats feel good about themselves. *(crossing upstage right to the book shelf)* They confuse enjoying the play with genuine civic engagement. If you really want to shake people up, put on a play endorsed by the NRA. They'll be screaming in the aisles, canceling subscriptions left and right.

HEIDI. I thought you were the money guy.

MIKE. *(sitting near her on the desk)* I'm not saying alienate the subscription base, I'm saying let's entice the ones who left the audience to return. Or appeal to young people. Let's put on a play that everyone likes.

(**MIKE** *examines the Hrosvitha book.*)

HEIDI. You should be producing on Broadway.

MIKE. You caught me. That's where I'm hoping to be. Very soon.

(**MIKE** *looks at the open script.*)

HEIDI. Yeah?

MIKE. *(with a finger to his lips)* Our secret.

HEIDI. Bit of a step up from usher.

MIKE. Hm?

HEIDI. Jim said you started out as an usher.

MIKE. …Yes. I did.

HEIDI. *(moving away from him)* Sorry. You don't want to talk about–

MIKE. No, it's okay. It's not something I'm in the habit of discussing. It was a long time ago. What do you want to know?

HEIDI. God, I'm embarrassed now.

MIKE. Don't be. I'm enjoying it. People don't usually ask me personal questions.

HEIDI. *(moving toward him)* Jim said it had something to do with your father.

(**MIKE** *crosses back to the book shelf, facing upstage.*)

...Was he forcing you to do something you didn't want?

MIKE. *(Turning down. Smiling.) Circumstances* were forcing me to do something I didn't want. My dad died when I was eighteen...My mom couldn't work, so...

HEIDI. I shouldn't have asked.

MIKE. ...You gonna reject that play?

HEIDI. I don't know. I'm not done yet. Jim tells me to reject it after ten pages, but I can't bring myself to do that.

MIKE. *(smiling)* Regular young Turk.

HEIDI. *(modestly)* I don't know about that...

MIKE. It's good. Change is good. Makes the place more efficient.

(**MIKE** *grabs an empty coffee cup from the book shelf. He sees an empty spiral notebook among the books. He takes it with his other hand.*)

HEIDI. *(sitting in* **JIM***s' chair)* I hope so.

(**MIKE** *throws away the empty cup and crosses above* **HEIDI**.*)*

MIKE. You know what you might want to do? If you see something happening in the office that you don't like, that you think needs to be changed, write it down.

HEIDI. Like a log?

MIKE. Yeah, just write down whatever you want changed. In a notebook. So you don't forget them.

HEIDI. What about Jim?

MIKE. I assume you've already talked to Jim about some of these things, right?

HEIDI. Some of them.

MIKE. And he wasn't–what–amenable? Right?

HEIDI. Right.

MIKE. So maybe here's how I can help you out. Not just you, but all of the playwrights who send their scripts to us. They deserve better, don't you think?

HEIDI. Definitely.

MIKE. Not all of them are bad, right? It's the good guys we're doing it for. But I can't help without something in writing, you understand?

HEIDI. No, I know.

MIKE. Can you do that?

HEIDI. I can do that.

MIKE. Then when you think you've got enough, maybe we can get together and address these issues.

HEIDI. Like a meeting?

MIKE. Like a meeting, like dinner… *(a beat)* You don't *have* to…

HEIDI. No, I *want* to. I want to. It's just, the money situation–

MIKE. Dinner's on me. Charge it to the theater. It's a business meeting, right?

HEIDI. I guess so.

MIKE. Okay?

HEIDI. –Yeah.

MIKE. Great. I'll call you, now that the phone is working, and set it up. –Let me know when Jim comes in.

(**MIKE** *crosses down left of desks.*)

HEIDI. *(standing)* Will do.

MIKE. Is this him–?

(*It is not, for* **TINA** *enters.*)

Sorry, Tina. Thought you were Jim.

TINA. Well, I'm not wearing make-up…

(**TINA** *puts her bag on Jim's desk.* **MIKE** *sits on the desk's edge.*)

MIKE. Ticket sales. Up, up, up. Am I right?

TINA. I don't give a damn about that. Where's Jim?

HEIDI. Any minute now.

TINA. That means nothing. When is he meeting with Janet?

HEIDI. Three.

MIKE. Any news on your friends?

TINA. They're coming.

MIKE. How many seats?

TINA. *(sitting in Heidi's chair)* Don't worry. It's a done deal.

MIKE. Nothing is done until you see it in print.

TINA. They've moved all my stuff into New York. This one will get there too.

MIKE. And the script is ready for them?

TINA. Why wouldn't it be ready?

> (TINA *removes a folder full of new pages from her bag. She puts the bag on the floor.*)

MIKE. All I want to hear. –Are you in the box office tonight?

HEIDI. Mm-hmm.

MIKE. Could you put aside five house seats for opening night under Niederbert?

HEIDI. *(Wow!)* Oh my God!

MIKE. Maybe you can use this, regarding that little matter we just talked about. *(placing the notebook on Heidi's desk)* –Who's on hold?

HEIDI. Oh God, I forgot.

> (MIKE *exits as* HEIDI *runs to the phone.*)

Hello? –Shoot.

> (HEIDI *hangs up.*)

TINA. What time is the meeting with Janet again?

HEIDI. Three.

TINA. *(half to herself)* I want him to have these before the meeting.

HEIDI. Literally any minute. He's usually in by now.

TINA. I'm gonna miss my train.

HEIDI. Is there anything I can help you with?

TINA. Can you be trusted?

HEIDI. Of course I can be trusted.

TINA. Can you? What the hell did you do to this place? It's neat.

HEIDI. I just put a few things away.

TINA. I don't *trust* neat. Especially in a literary office. *(standing and crossing downstage left)* What is that? Air freshener?

HEIDI. Just a little–

TINA. I don't trust that smell in a dramaturg. A dramaturg's gotta smell like cigarettes, coffee, moldy paper, and sweat.

HEIDI. Well, I used to smoke…

TINA. *(gathering her things)* I'll come back tomorrow.

> *(**TINA** starts to exit.)*

HEIDI. Don't go.

> *(**HEIDI** grabs a coffee cup from the trash. She dips her finger into the cup and applies some coffee behind her ears like perfume. She crosses to **TINA** and offers her neck to smell.)*

HEIDI. How's that?

TINA. …You're a nut. *(a fractional beat)* I can trust a nut. Give these to Jim when he comes in.

> *(**TINA** hands a folder to **HEIDI**. **HEIDI** begins poring through it.)*

HEIDI. New pages?

TINA. I did everything he asked. I'm getting kinder in my old age.

> *(**TINA** removes sunglasses from her bag.)*

HEIDI. I gotta tell you, I loved your play.

TINA. *(putting on the sunglasses)* Yeah, well, I had to write something. Keeps me from being alone with my thoughts. Too depressing.

(**TINA** *turns to exit.*)

HEIDI. I directed *Woman of the Corn* in college.

TINA. God, I can't bear that play anymore.

(**TINA** *crosses to her poster and tilts it again.*)

HEIDI. I think you're one of the few contemporary playwrights whose work will survive.

TINA. Survive what?

HEIDI. You know, last. Forever.

TINA. Why do you think that?

(**HEIDI** *crosses downstage left, looking through the new
pages.*)

HEIDI. The emotional range. It's extraordinary. Even when
we're laughing, it's tinged with such sadness. And the
truths about women. They're universal, they're– What
about the monologue in act two? What happened to
it?

TINA. (*crossing to* **HEIDI**) Cut. Jim didn't like it.

HEIDI. Janet's the director, what did she say?

TINA. She left it up to me.

HEIDI. No, you have to put it back in.

TINA. Jim thinks–

HEIDI. Look, personally? I don't think Jim knows what he's
doing. I know your work. I studied you in school. That
monologue is what makes this a Tina Fike play.

TINA. (*crossing downstage right*) It doesn't affect the plot.

HEIDI. But *thematically* it encapsulates your vision for the
role of women in world culture. All of your plays have
tangential monologues like this, but this one gives the
entire canon closure.

TINA. (*almost a grunt*) Hmp.

HEIDI. It spoke to me as a woman–it speaks to all women.
Jim's not going to understand that. He's not going to
see what that monologue means because he's a man.
I'm surprised Janet would let him even consider cutting it.

TINA. With Mike breathing down her neck, Janet's more worried about losing money than losing six pages of text.

HEIDI. That doesn't concern you, though, does it?

(JIM *enters, heading straight for the desk.* HEIDI *crosses upstage with the folder.*)

JIM. Hello hello. Tina. I'm sorry. Forgive me. I love you. You're brilliant. You're wonderful. You're talented. I'm late. I know. I promised. I'm sorry. Doctors. Changes?

TINA. Yeah, let me just…

(TINA *takes the folder from* HEIDI. *She removes the page wherein the monologue is cut. She folds it up and hands the manilla folder to* JIM.)

JIM. Thank you, Dumpling. I'm meeting with Janet today at four–

HEIDI. Three.

JIM. Look, I set the alarm. And we will integrate all of it as soon as we can.

(JIM *sits at the desk and begins to add the changes to his script.*)

TINA. I'm still undecided about Two-five.

JIM. *(warning a child)* …The monologue? Tina, we talked about this. Don't make me show mister angry face.

TINA. I'm thinking it over.

JIM. A week from today. That's when we open. Watch the previews. It's dragging the show.

TINA. It's not dragging the show.

JIM. Come on, Tina, this is me you're talking to.

TINA. I'm not saying I won't cut it. I'm saying I need to think about it. *(crossing to the exit)* I'm late for my train.

JIM. *(standing)* Let me show you out.

TINA. Stop showing me out. I don't need to be shown out. It's not like I'll get lost between here and the train station. It's just across the way. I don't have Alzheimer's.

JIM. But I hear it strikes suddenly.

TINA. *(indicating* **HEIDI***)* Why doesn't *she* sit in on our meetings?

JIM. She does. You just don't notice her because you need to be shown out.

*(***TINA*** makes a dismissive gesture at ***JIM*** and exits.)*

JIM. God, what got into that old hag? Somebody increase her dosage? *(removing his jacket and draping it over a chair)* I thought we had an agreement. Why did she change her mind about the monologue? –Mail?

HEIDI. Mm-hmm.

*(***JIM*** tosses the mail into the trash without a glance.)*

JIM. Oops.

*(***JIM*** sits, returning to work. ***HEIDI*** sighs and takes the mail out of the trash. The phone rings.)*

HEIDI. That's probably the guy from before. Talk to him. I need to get a script report.

*(***HEIDI*** exits down right. ***JIM*** picks up the phone and holds his nose, affecting the nasal voice of a recorded operator.)*

JIM. If you wish to make a call, please hang up and dial again. …If you wish to make a call, pl–

*(The caller has hung up. ***JIM*** does the same. ***HEIDI*** enters with the script report.)*

HEIDI. What happened?

JIM. I don't know. He hung up.

*(The phone rings. ***HEIDI*** crosses to it.)*

What a morning. I'll be in conference.

HEIDI. Mike wants to see you.

JIM. *(singsong)* Conference. Conference!

*(***JIM*** grabs Heidi's coffee cup and exits into the conference room with the script and the folder of changes. ***HEIDI*** answers the phone.)*

HEIDI. Literary. ...Hi, yes, I'm sorry...No, I apologize, I–

JIM. *(entering)* Shhh!

> *(**JIM** mouths "Conference" and exits into the conference room, slamming the door. **HEIDI** glares after him.)*

HEIDI. Yeah, I have the report right here. What did you want to know?

> *(**HEIDI** sits. As she listens, **HEIDI** discovers the notebook that Mike gave her. She picks it up and examines it, looking after **JIM**.)*

...I'm sorry, could you repeat that? ...Right.

> *(**HEIDI** continues with the phone call as the lights fade. Audio for the scene change begins.)*

Scene Change 3

(Ostensibly, this is a radio interview.)

HOST. You've mentioned the action of a play many times now. What exactly is that?

PLAYWRIGHT. Well–

HOST. Because when I think of action in the movies, it's usually a car chase or an explosion, am I right?

PLAYWRIGHT. Well, yeah, that's–

(They share a laugh.)

HOST. And you don't have those in plays!

PLAYWRIGHT. No.

HOST. But I mean, have you thought about it?

PLAYWRIGHT. What.

HOST. Putting a car chase in your play?

PLAYWRIGHT. Putting–?

HOST. Yeah, just to shake things up. Make it more appealing to the men being dragged there by their wives.

PLAYWRIGHT. Well–

HOST. No? Why not?

PLAYWRIGHT. ...Uh– Theater's a live event.

HOST. And Nascar isn't?

(pause)

PLAYWRIGHT. Yeah, but I don't think a car chase–

HOST. Just trying to help. Think about it. Let's take a caller. Gary from Peekskill, you're on the air.

(lights up on scene four)

Scene 4

(**HEIDI** *sits at her desk, writing in her notebook and drinking coffee.* **JIM** *sits in front of his desk, reading a script. Except for the typing, all is quiet as the lights come up.* **JIM** *laughs at the script and shakes his head.*)

JIM. Oh God.

(**HEIDI** *begins typing on her laptop.* **JIM** *reads some more and again laughs and shakes his head.*)

Oh God.

HEIDI. Keeper?

JIM. Crapper. Definitely a crapper. Five pages, handwritten, bound by a staple and he's hoping it will go to Broadway. The only way this thing will get to New York is if it arrives as landfill!

HEIDI. Why are *you* reading scripts?

JIM. Joey sneaks in tomorrow for his monthly clandestine mail pick-up.

(*Small beat as* **JIM** *returns to the script.* **HEIDI** *checks her purse.*)

HEIDI. Do you have a dollar I could borrow?

JIM. (*removing a dollar from his wallet*) Planning to eat tonight?

HEIDI. Actually, someone's buying me dinner.

JIM. A date? Who gave you the right to a social life?

HEIDI. It's not a date.

JIM. Then what?

HEIDI. None of your business.

JIM. That ugly? Order the lobster.

HEIDI. It's not a date.

JIM. (*taunting her with the dollar*) Come on. If you want Mr. Washington, you gotta fess up. At least tell me what the dollar's for.

HEIDI. If you must know. The dollar is for toilet paper. Happy now?

(**JIM** *gives her a dollar*)

JIM. Keep it.

HEIDI. I'll pay it back.

JIM. Keep it.

HEIDI. Thanks.

(**HEIDI** *types.* **JIM** *looks over her shoulder.*)

JIM. Script report?

HEIDI. Mm-hmm.

JIM. Who's the playwright?

HEIDI. John Morogiello.

JIM. Oh God! Throw it away! ...This one too.

(**JIM** *hands the handwritten script to* **HEIDI.** *He takes a new one from one of the piles and returns to his desk.*)

HEIDI. I'd like to read it first.

JIM. Let it be payback for the hairdresser play.

HEIDI. *(no longer typing)* Did you get to it?

JIM. I did.

HEIDI. *(standing)* And you didn't tell me? You must have hated it.

(**HEIDI** *crosses down left*)

JIM. If I hated it, I would have rubbed your nose in it.

HEIDI. *(turning to him)* You liked it?

JIM. It was hilarious. Coffee spewing hilarity.

HEIDI. Yeah, but in the end–

JIM. Exquisite. I mean, I wasn't in tears–

HEIDI. *(crossing right)* But with a little work–

JIM. With a little work–

HEIDI. *(crossing to Jim's desk)* Did you like when they were watching Mildred Pierce?

JIM. And the mom comes in–?

HEIDI. Wondering what's so funny!

JIM. And they're just laughing at it like a couple of old queens!

(JIM *emits a screaming cackle.*)

HEIDI. So, you believe me now.

JIM. I believe you.

HEIDI. I wasn't out of my mind.

JIM. Not right then, no. Thank you for recommending it.

HEIDI. *(crossing down right)* I can't wait to see what Joey says about it.

JIM. Actually, he won't have a chance. I sent it back to the playwright.

HEIDI. …What??? Why?

JIM. It's a better than average AIDS play that adds nothing new to the genre. Joey wouldn't have liked it.

HEIDI. But that's his decision.

JIM. If I can make it for him, I don't see why I should waste his time.

HEIDI. *(crossing to Jim's desk)* Because that's his job. He's being paid to read good scripts.

JIM. No, he's being paid to let us use his name on our let-terhead. We've got Janet and we've got Joey, that's what makes us a nationally renowned theater. Without them, it's just "We've got a barn, let's put on a show."

HEIDI. *(crossing down left)* Somehow I don't think Joey would resign over one script.

JIM. Patrick Donnelly is nobody. He doesn't even have an agent.

HEIDI. One of the best plays I ever saw had no agent. It was called *Hamlet.*

JIM. *(crossing to* HEIDI.*)* I understand you're upset. The play had merit. *(crossing down right)* And if we were some tiny blackbox on the third floor of an urban ware-house, I would agree with you. But at this level, our job is not to promote beginners, but to protect the veter-ans *from* those beginners.

HEIDI. That is not what we're here for. Read the subscrip-tion brochures, we brag all over that we do new plays.

JIM. *(grabbing a script from the down right pile)* Yes, but read who wrote the new plays: Lynn Nottage, Martin McDonagh, Tina Fike. They're veterans. Not one unknown up there. Unknowns don't sell tickets.

HEIDI. *(stepping toward* **JIM***)* A good play is a good play.

JIM. Thank you, Gertrude Stein. But the public don't consider a *new* play to be a *good* play. They want a guarantee that our new plays won't be like those other new plays. We provide that guarantee by only producing new plays by established writers.

*(***JIM*** puts the script back on the pile and heads up right.* **HEIDI** *crosses down left.)*

HEIDI. Only?

JIM. Only.

HEIDI. *(leaning on her desk)* No play from this office has ever made it to production?

JIM. *(leaning on his desk)* I know. Scales. Blop! *(***JIM*** *mimes scales falling from* **HEIDI***'s eyes. He crosses above the desk.)* Audiences don't want plays. They want events: gay cats singing and dancing at a Dublin bar mitzvah.

HEIDI. *(crossing right)* How did we get Tina's play?

JIM. The same way we always do: She lives next door to Janet. Tina's plays never spend a nanosecond in this office. She knows somebody. It's the same with dramaturgs. I worked in Boston when Tina was in residence. When she set up shop here, I followed.

HEIDI. What about in–?

JIM. *(crossing down right to* **HEIDI***)* No unknown playwrights were being done in Boston either. That's the way it works everywhere.

HEIDI. It's not like that everywhere.

JIM. It is.

HEIDI. Have you worked everywhere?

JIM. It has been true enough in my experience for me to extrapolate: everywhere.

(JIM *crosses to the desk and grabs his cigarettes.*)

HEIDI. *(following* JIM*)* Have you ever considered that it's not the theaters that have such a jaded, elitist attitude, but you?

JIM. Yes, that's exactly it. I'm the bad guy.

(HEIDI *grabs Jim's lighter and crosses down left.*)

HEIDI. Maybe you are, Jim. Every day: you come in late, you're rude, you're sloppy.

(JIM *follows, taking the lighter back.*)

JIM. And I smoke in a non-smoking zone! I'm Beelzebub! …Let's get back to the point–

(JIM *sits at his desk and fails to light the cigarette.*)

HEIDI. Everything about you is a mess. You say it yourself all the time, but you don't lift a finger to change it.

JIM. *(preening)* Some things cannot be changed.

HEIDI. *(stepping toward him)* Of course they can't, if you just sit there and whine about them. You've got to do something. Even a small gesture like giving *Requiem for a Hairdresser* to Joey Tilson could be the beginning of a revolution.

(JIM *fails to light the cigarette again.*)

JIM. It's too late.

HEIDI. It's not too late.

JIM. It is for Patrick Donnelly, the mail already came.

HEIDI. There are theaters that encourage young playwrights. I know, because new ones continually emerge.

JIM. Perhaps you should intern at one of them.

(JIM *tries the lighter again.*)

HEIDI. But we could be that theater, Jim. We could be the ones bearing the banner for a new American drama.

JIM. Spare me.

HEIDI. Things have got to change here.

JIM. *(putting the lighter down)* And who are you?

HEIDI. If you don't give these playwrights the respect they deserve, I'm gonna act independently of you.

JIM. You're an intern!!! What the fuck kind of power trip are you on? You can't do anything.

HEIDI. *(sitting at her desk)* I already have.

JIM. *(standing with lighter and cigarette)* Have you. Goody, goody.

HEIDI. You want to know what I did?

JIM. *(preparing to exit)* Not really.

HEIDI. I told Tina to keep the monologue in act two.

JIM. …Don't be silly.

HEIDI. She had agreed to cut it, but I convinced her not to.

(**HEIDI** *straightens the poster and sits again.*)

JIM. …Are you out of your mind!?

HEIDI. That monologue is an intrinsic element of the Tina Fike canon.

JIM. It's a rant.

HEIDI. There's nothing wrong with a rant.

JIM. Yes, there is. Audiences won't sit through proselytizing anymore. It's too last century!

HEIDI. I sit through proselytizing every day. "Plot is dead. I'm the great white structure hunter."

(**JIM** *crosses down right.*)

JIM. That's in here. No one in his right mind would put *this* on stage!

HEIDI. You don't know Tina's work like I do.

JIM. *(stepping toward* **HEIDI***)* I'm her dramaturg! Nobody knows her better than I. You had no right or authority to discuss revisions with my playwright.

HEIDI. She doesn't belong to you.

JIM. *(crossing down right)* Yes, she does. I turged her last three shows before they got to New York. I spent the last ten years trying to gain her trust. That's my job; to get them to put their faith in me. You think you can just come in here and bark orders and everyone will snap to attention? It doesn't work that way. Nobody will listen to you.

HEIDI. Tina did.

(**JIM** *crosses to* **HEIDI.**)

JIM. Because you told her not to do something she didn't want to do anyway! Do you know how many playwrights it takes to change a light bulb? "Change? Who said anything about a change?"

(**HEIDI** *stands and crosses down left.*)

HEIDI. You weren't pointing Tina in the direction of self-discovery; you were just dictating your own personal will. That monologue brings closure to her themes of woman as universal mother. The whole script is one of her best.

JIM. But it could be *better.* You can hear the coughing in the audience, the shifting in the seats. The distress and boredom are palpable.

HEIDI. It's worth it.

JIM. It's worth it to have Charles Isherwood's butt fall asleep?

(*Author's note: The director is free to substitute the name of any other critic from* The New York Times *or locally who is equally prone to posterior somnolence.*)

HEIDI. Yes! A hundred years from now, people will be grateful for this final key to the door of Tina Fike's work. (**HEIDI** *crosses down right.*) Students will study our conversation and marvel at the dramaturgical miscarriage we narrowly avoided.

JIM. (*crossing above his desk*) Students study what an audience avoids. People's jobs are at stake here! People's lives!

HEIDI. (*moving suddenly to the other side of Jim's desk*) Tina and I will fight you for that monologue with all of our strength. The cause of art is sacred. You cannot talk of it in terms of "worth."

(a beat)

JIM. Okay. I am going to step outside now. I am going to walk off my anger. Recite the most calming mantra I can recall. And then I am going to bash my head repeatedly against the wall, because I am better off doing that than trying to teach you how to become a dramaturg.

(JIM slowly starts to exit with cigarette and lighter. HEIDI crosses to him. Her voice stops him.)

HEIDI. I didn't do it to upset you. It's just that I know I'm right.

JIM. You are no longer sitting in on my meetings with Tina and Janet.

(Again JIM heads toward the door, only to be stopped by HEIDI's line.)

HEIDI. Tina wants me there.

JIM. But I don't.

HEIDI. *(sitting at her desk)* Fine, I won't come. We open tomorrow anyway. What's one meeting?

JIM. From now on, you do things my way, or you go. The only reason you're still here at all is because I desperately need the help and no one else will get me coffee.

(A third time JIM heads toward the door. HEIDI steps toward JIM and stops him with her line.)

HEIDI. I won't stop. I have a whole notebook–.

JIM. Jesus Christ! You won't even grant me an exit line!?

(JIM exits angrily, slamming the door. HEIDI grabs a cigarette from Jim's pack. She puts it in her mouth as MIKE enters.)

MIKE. Hey.

HEIDI. Almost ready.

MIKE. There's no smoking.

HEIDI. *(putting the cigarette down)* Sorry. I get so tempted when Jim does it.

(**HEIDI** *crosses to her bag.*)

MIKE. Big day tomorrow.

HEIDI. The Niederberts still coming?

MIKE. Fifth row center. If I make the right play for them? Who knows.

HEIDI. *(crossing to* **MIKE***)* All set.

MIKE. You got the book?

HEIDI. Ah, thanks.

(*She pulls the notebook from the desk and hands it to* **MIKE***.*)

Here you go.

MIKE. *(thumbing through it)* A lot in here.

HEIDI. Well, a lot needs to be changed. *(closing the book to get his attention)* Let's get dinner.

MIKE. After you.

(**HEIDI** *exits.* **MIKE** *looks back into the office, smiles, and turns off the lights as he exits with the notebook. The act curtain falls.*)

ACT TWO

(In the darkness jaunty music is heard, like something from an educational film of the early seventies.)

NARRATOR. *(as happy and jaunty as the music)* Writing a play is easy! Just ask Alan Ayckbourn: he's written thousands of them, with no discernable talent whatsoever!

How does he do it, you ask? He employs a secret known to only the most successful modern playwrights. It's called "formulaic plotting." Just follow the four simple steps on this CD.

Step One: Buy some paper.

Step Two: Write a play on it. Preferably something really good.

Step Three: Mail your play to a theater.

Step Four: Sit back and wait for the offers to pour in! These four steps could put you on the road to Broadway.

(jaunty music fades as the lights come up on...)

Scene 1

(A gift box of black label scotch is on the desk. JIM *and* TINA *are drinking and laughing.* TINA *is dressed nicely for opening night.* JIM *looks the same except for a cream scarf draped around his neck.)*

TINA. That's no opening night disaster. You remember the Baltimore story?

JIM. Which one?

TINA. With the gun?

JIM. Never heard it.

TINA. Never? It's my only story.

JIM. *(sitting at his desk)* But you only tell it when I'm drinking, you can't expect me to remember–

TINA. *(dramatically leaning against the upstage wall)* So I'm in Baltimore.

JIM. When?

TINA. *(crossing down left)* Before your time. I was just starting out, and some small theater there decides to produce some one-act of mine which I have since suppressed. Anyway, what's supposed to happen. Peter is center, with a gun pointed right at Bob's head. You're Bob. *(pointing her fingers, like a gun, at* JIM*)* I say, "Who told you that?" And you say, "Mary." So Peter's supposed to turn and bang, Mary's dead. That's what's supposed to happen.

*(*TINA *has turned one hundred eighty degrees and "shot" the imaginary Mary behind her.)*

JIM. Mm-hmm.

TINA. Opening night here's what actually occured: *(*TINA *points at* JIM*.)* "Who told you that?" "Mary." BANG!

(The "gun" is still pointed at JIM*, who is enjoying this immensely.)*

JIM. Oh God, no!

TINA. There's a pause, and you can see the panic in the eyes of the actors. They start...

(TINA *furtively looks around for assistance.* JIM *laughs.*)

Mary falls dead.

(TINA *gestures behind her.* JIM *laughs.*)

And they went on with the play! *That's* a disaster. I can't believe you never heard that story.

(TINA *crosses down right.*)

JIM. Are you kidding? I hear it three times a year! I'm sucking up to you, you old hag.

(TINA *is amused by this.*)

TINA. It's about fucking time. Strike a little fear in your heart. You haven't been sufficiently afraid of me in years. I like when they're afraid of me. I can mess with them that way.

JIM. If I ever need to be scared, I'll just watch your second act.

TINA. That's what really frightens you. *Who,* I should say.

(TINA *crosses to the desk and holds out her empty glass.* JIM *stands to fill it.*)

I'll give you fifty bucks for what's-her-name.

JIM. Who.

TINA. *(crossing down right)* The intern.

JIM. You're taking her advice and you don't even know her name!

TINA. What do I need her name for?

JIM. *(refilling his own glass)* Aren't we cheap.

TINA. *(crossing left)* Think she'd be interested?

JIM. Personally or professionally?

TINA. Personally.

JIM. She may not be a "member of the fold."

TINA. You know why I like her? *(crossing up left)* –She reminds me of somebody.

JIM. She does not.

TINA. *(crossing down left)* You remember. In Boston? "Oooh, Ms. Fike, I'm so excited to be working with you."

JIM. *(crossing to* **TINA***)* That's not what I said.

TINA. "You're just so fabulous!"

JIM. Well, you *are* fabulous. How could I help myself?

TINA. You're sucking up again.

JIM. *(crossing down right)* Isn't that why you're so interested in her? Isn't that what you want?

TINA. In a lover, sure. Not in a dramaturg.

JIM. Then why did you keep the monologue?

TINA. *(sitting in Jim's chair)* Because I like the monologue. …And I like her.

JIM. You like her youth.

TINA. And you don't.

JIM. No, I don't.

TINA. Why not?

JIM. Because I've lived her youth. Impatient idealism leads two ways. If you're lucky, it leads to incredible success and everyone marvels at your brilliance. If you're not, it leads to failure and bitterness. Most people are out to destroy her kind of attitude.

TINA. Including you, it sounds like.

JIM. *(crossing up right)* I'm trying to ease her gently into the role of jaded cog in the theatrical machine. I don't want her fall to be too painful.

TINA. I like that she doesn't take any shit.

JIM. Well, she doesn't take it from me, but that's the way I work. If the right person brought her a plateful, she'd taste it and pretend to like it like the rest of us. Then they'll start feeding her so much, she'll be gagging on the great clumps. *Then* she'll be a dramaturg, and all that stuff you see in her will be gone.

(**JIM** *sits at Heidi's desk.*)

TINA. You never know, she may be right.

JIM. About what?

TINA. About my monologue. About how things should be done around here.

(**MIKE** *enters, dressed in a fancy suit. He carries an envelope.*)

MIKE. Hey.

JIM. *(standing)* The boss! Hide the bottle!

MIKE. Already celebrating? The play hasn't even started.

JIM. Care to join us in an opening night toast?

MIKE. I just came to drop this off.

(**MIKE** *hands* **JIM** *the envelope.*)

JIM. Early Christmas bonus?

(**JIM** *crosses upstage right and sits on the edge of the desk.*)

MIKE. *(to* **TINA***)* Janet and I just got back from dinner with your friends.

TINA. Yeah?

MIKE. They're excited about the play.

TINA. Great.

MIKE. I talked their ears off.

TINA. I'll apologize later.

MIKE. What does that mean?

JIM. *(offering the bottle)* You sure you wouldn't like to–

MIKE. No, thanks. Not under the circumstances. Where's Heidi?

JIM. Box office tonight. Then primp for the party.

MIKE. Tina, when you get a chance, they're looking for you downstairs.

TINA. I doubt they'll find me.

MIKE. Okay. …Well…break a leg.

TINA. Fuck off. That's actors.

(**MIKE** *exits.*)

JIM. What circumstances is he talking about?

(TINA shrugs. JIM opens the envelope. Before he can remove the note, his watch alarm beeps. He puts the envelope down, stands, and takes his pills with the alcohol over the following.)

JIM. This is my life now. All day, every day. I don't eat anymore. I'm not hungry. I'm too stuffed with meds.

TINA. How are you doing?

JIM. A year undetectable. You can't get rid of me that easily. It's just a pain in the ass.

TINA. …What time is it?

JIM. Half hour.

TINA. *(standing)* I better shmooze with the money.

(TINA puts on her shoes downstage of desk)

JIM. I'll be down in a bit.

TINA. One more. *(pouring a shot for herself and toasting JIM)* Salud.

(She knocks back the shot, puts down the glass, and exits. JIM gazes at the gift box with affection and places it in the trash. He puts the top back on the scotch bottle. He sweeps the pill bottles into the drawer and closes it in one fluid motion. He remembers the envelope, pulls the note from it and reads. He palls.)

JIM. Oh my God.

(The lights fade. Party sounds rise.)

Scene 2

(Later that night. The office is dark. Light spills in from outside the brown window. A shaft of light from the hall pierces the glass of the door. HEIDI pokes her head through the door.)

HEIDI. Jim?

(She flips on the lights as the sound fades. HEIDI and MIKE enter, still garbed in opening night formality, carrying plastic cups. HEIDI hands her cup to MIKE, crosses to the conference room, and peers inside. She turns back to MIKE, crossing up right of the desk.)

…Nobody here.

MIKE. This is good. I mean, I love parties–

(MIKE sits at Jim's desk.)

HEIDI. No, I agree. The noise was getting to me too.

MIKE. I wanted to talk to the Niederberts, but I couldn't even hear myself think.

HEIDI. Everyone was celebrating a hit.

MIKE. Or it's like that story where the people party while the plague is killing everyone outside.

HEIDI. *The Masque of the Red Death.*

MIKE. Is that it?

HEIDI. *The Decameron?*

MIKE. It doesn't matter. We'll see when the reviews come out.

HEIDI. *(crossing down right)* You want to wait up all night for them, like in a Kaufman play?

MIKE. They're not gonna be out for a couple days.

HEIDI. *(turning away from MIKE)* If the play is a hit, are you still planning to jump ship?

MIKE. That's the only way I'll be *able* to jump ship. If it fails, I'm going down like a deck steward on the Titanic. We all are.

HEIDI. I guess Renee's job would be out of the question then?

MIKE. That's already taken care of.

HEIDI. Did she give notice?

MIKE. I can't say anymore. It will ruin the surprise.

HEIDI. *(crossing to the desk)* Now I'm intrigued.

MIKE. *(smiling)* Change the subject.

HEIDI. *(crossing down left)* So how come I'm dying to break in here, and you're dying to get out?

MIKE. That's an easy one. You're just starting out. For me, it's time to move on.

HEIDI. Why?

MIKE. Money.

HEIDI. I'm so sick of money. There's more to life than money.

MIKE. Yeah. But money helps you get that "more to life."

HEIDI. *(crossing upstage left, leaning on wall)* You sound like my dad now.

MIKE. *(pouring some of **JIM**'s scotch in their cups)* Think about it. What's "more to life?" Art, family, love, crap like that, right? You think we could have done Tina's play without money? Raising a family takes money too. As does love. Even the church has a collection plate.

HEIDI. I guess it depends on your definition of "more to life."

MIKE. What's your definition?

*(**MIKE** hands **HEIDI** a cup.)*

HEIDI. I don't know. We lived on the border between upper middle class and wealthy. There was no inner life to be nurtured in any of us, just autocratic dictates to be carried out. My dad insisted that pursuit of wealth was to be my only concern. My mom started drinking. My brother ran away. All the money in the world didn't make us happy.

MIKE. *(smiling)* I'm sorry your family caused you such pain and bitterness. I am, really. But I mean it when I say you're full of shit.

HEIDI. *(pushing his chair)* No, you're full of shit.

MIKE. Oh, boo hoo, a Volvo for my sixteenth birthday? I wanted a Mercedes.

HEIDI. *(crossing left)* It wasn't like that. Life at home sucked. I'm much happier now, being a member of the working poor.

MIKE. You're young, single, over-educated. What kind of responsibilities do you have?

HEIDI. You try living in this town on minimum wage.

MIKE. *(smiling)* I have. And I supported my mom in a wheelchair with it. Nursed her and paid her medical bills with a part time job instead of going to college. No insurance, no savings. Where was my "more to life?"

HEIDI. What did you do?

*(**HEIDI** sits on the edge of her desk.)*

MIKE. What else *could* I do? I set a goal, worked hard, got to know the right people, taught myself a few things. And eventually I rose up the ladder and the money came. *Then* I could appreciate that there was more to life.

HEIDI. I'm sorry.

*(**MIKE** stands, leaving his cup on the desk, moving right.)*

MIKE. *(smiling)* Everyone's got a sob story. I'm not trying to play "can you top this?" I'm just laying out the facts. *(crossing upstage right)* I'm doing pretty good, but I've gone as far as I can go here and I'm not even forty yet. It's time to lace up those dancing shoes.

HEIDI. I know. It's just one more illusion shattered.

MIKE. What? That money *can* make people happy? That poor people aren't as happy as that old English guy always made them out to be?

HEIDI. Who?

MIKE. *(crossing down right)* The guy who wrote the books.

HEIDI. Dickens?

MIKE. Is it?

HEIDI. It doesn't matter.

> *(**MIKE** sits on the desk beside **HEIDI**. He speaks softly, as though imparting true wisdom.)*

MIKE. You don't have to do what your dad says. Do what *you* want. You see a goal, you reach out for it and don't let anybody tell you no.

HEIDI. That's good advice.

MIKE. It's how I've lived my life. And based on what you've told me, I think it's how you've lived your life too.

HEIDI. *(standing)* …We're a lot alike.

MIKE. *(standing and leaning in)* I take that as a compliment.

> *(a lull in the conversation)*

HEIDI. We should probably get back to the party.

> *(**HEIDI** starts to cross to the door, but **MIKE** gently touches her arm to stop her. She turns to him. He kisses her. As the kiss becomes desperately passionate, they awkwardly exit into the conference chamber, grappling at each other's clothes and perhaps bumping into the desk. A pause. **JIM** staggers on through the other door. He takes the pill bottles from his desk drawer and places them on the desk. He opens the scotch and cleans one of the glasses on his desk with his scarf. He pours the scotch but misses the glass. He uses a script as a sponge to soak up the spill, knocking over the pencil holder. **JIM** takes the pills, swigging directly from the scotch bottle as a soft, clandestine grunt or moan is heard from the conference chamber. **JIM** looks around, bewildered. A beat. A similar noise is heard.)*

JIM. Hello?!

> *(The noise of scurrying, and cursing, and searching for clothes comes from the conference chamber. **JIM** crosses to the chamber, peering in.)*

JIM. Who is th–OH MY GOD!

(*JIM turns away from the chamber, from which more noises may be heard. He ends up upstage center.* **MIKE** *enters with his tie and jacket slung over his arm. He is tucking in his shirt and betrays no embarrassment. He smiles at* **JIM.**)

MIKE. (*a matter of fact greeting*) Jim…Didn't expect you to be here.

JIM. Obviously.

MIKE. (*a nod of the head toward the conference room door*) You should try it sometime.

(**MIKE** *exits.* **HEIDI** *enters, only slightly more put together than was* **MIKE.** *She is mortified.*)

HEIDI. I am so sorry. I didn't expect–

JIM. (*overlapping*) –expect me to be here. I know.

HEIDI. We got carried away.

JIM. What do I care? Fuck Big Mike Braschi whenever you want. Why do they call him "Big Mike" anyway?

HEIDI. You're mad at me. I understand.

JIM. I don't give a shit about you. I'm mad at me.

HEIDI. You didn't do anything.

JIM. (*crossing down right*) And therein lies the rub! You and Mike Braschi? That certainly explains a lot.

HEIDI. (*countering to upstage center*) It's not like we planned this.

JIM. Please. You know damn well who you were really fucking in there.

HEIDI. Mike? He's not as bad as you think.

JIM. (*advancing on* **HEIDI**) Not Mike Braschi! Me! You were fucking *me* in there! Ever since you got here, you have done nothing but fuck me!

HEIDI. (*escaping down left*) I never did anything to you!

JIM. (*countering to up center*) Then why did I lose my job?!

(*A stunned silence.* **JIM** *moves center.*)

Mike Braschi fired me! …*You* fired me!

HEIDI. Jim, I had nothing to do with this.

(*JIM angrily forces Mike's notice of termination on her. She reads it.*)

JIM. ...It says he has written evidence of my incompetence and dereliction. Where did he get written evidence?

HEIDI. ...God.

JIM. Were you keeping a list of complaints against me?

HEIDI. ...I didn't think–

(*In a rage, JIM slaps a pile of scripts off his desk.*)

I had no idea it would lead to this.

(*JIM subsides into weeping.*)

JIM. Why?

HEIDI. I don't know.

(*JIM crosses upstage center*)

JIM. For *Requiem for a Hairdresser*? My entire career for one play?

HEIDI. I-I thought it would help me get Renee's job.

JIM. Do you know how long I worked to get where I am? How hard?

HEIDI. (*crossing up right*) Another theater will snap you up in no time.

JIM. I was fired for incompetence. Dramaturgy jobs don't just sprout up–like weedy interns. How will I afford my meds? (*crossing down right*) –This office is all I have. There's no one in my life beyond that door. No family, cat, friends. They all liked my partner better, and when he died, everyone kind of–. I haven't had a hug in years. (*crossing down center*) Can you imagine what that's like? No physical human contact beyond a hand-shake... All I have is a mountain of bad scripts. I wake up, they're all over my house. I come to work, they're all over the office. You understand now why I am jaded and bitter and sorry for myself? I'm dead now. You killed me.

(The facade drops. JIM *slowly falls to his knees, weeping.* HEIDI *tries to comfort him with her words, without crossing to him.)*

HEIDI. ...I'm–I'm going to talk to Mike. I'm going to get you your job back.

(A beat. HEIDI *hesitantly crosses to* JIM *and kneels beside him. She hugs him as the lights fade. Soft music underscores the scene change.)*

Scene 3

(The next morning. **HEIDI** *is asleep in one of the chairs, using* **JIM***'s jacket as a blanket. Heidi's nice clothes and hair from the previous night are thoroughly rumpled. Noise from the conference room.* **HEIDI***'s head droops too far, waking her up. She looks around.* **JIM** *enters from the conference room. He too is wearing yesterday's rumpled clothes. Pause.)*

HEIDI. You're awake.

*(***JIM** *nods.* **HEIDI** *stands, leaving the jacket on the chair.)*

How are you feeling?

*(***JIM** *shrugs.)*

…Not hung over at all?

JIM. No.

HEIDI. …I cleaned up the mess. It wasn't too bad. Luckily most of it went into the wastebasket.

JIM. Thank you.

(A beat. **JIM** *grabs the jacket from the chair. He crosses down left.)*

HEIDI. Still mad?

JIM. *(stopping)* What time is it?

HEIDI *(looking at her watch)* Oh, God, it's time for work– well… I didn't mean it like–Jim…

*(***JIM** *exits.* **HEIDI** *sighs and begins to straighten the office.* **MIKE** *enters. He is wearing new clothes.)*

MIKE. Hey, you're in, good. I thought I saw your bike out there. Jesus. It smells awful in here.

*(***HEIDI** *crosses up left. She sprays air freshener.)*

HEIDI. Jim was sick.

*(***HEIDI** *sprays air freshener.* **MIKE** *gets a good look at her. He smiles.)*

MIKE. Didn't you go home at all?

(**HEIDI** *puts the scotch in* **JIM**'s *desk. She puts away his pill bottles.*)

HEIDI. I couldn't leave him alone.

MIKE. Guess what. I got the call. This morning, at home. First thing. The Niederberts are taking the production to New York! How about that?

(**HEIDI** *cleans* **JIM**'s *desk top with a paper towel.*)

HEIDI. Well, it's great for the theater.

MIKE. Forget the theater, it's great for me. I'm out of here.

HEIDI. They want you for the transfer?

MIKE. *(sitting at Heidi's desk)* Who else knows the ins and outs of this show? The economic pitfalls? And once I'm there I start doing other stuff. Making my presence known, getting in good with the guys in charge. Then I just stab some weakling higher-up in the back, and I'm in. You know how it's done.

HEIDI. *(twinge)* Yeah, I know.

MIKE. I thought you'd be happier. Is it last night? –I shouldn't have ran out. I know. I just figured the moment was gone.

(*He can see that he has guessed incorrectly.*)

You're sad 'cause I'm leaving. It doesn't have to be the end, we can still–

(*Again he is wrong.*)

What.

HEIDI. You fired Jim.

MIKE. Yeah. So?

HEIDI. …That's all you're going to say?

MIKE. The theater could only send one of us to New York. I needed to make sure it was me.

HEIDI. How could you be so selfish?

(**MIKE** *stands and crosses to* **HEIDI.**)

MIKE. I get it now. …Yes. The job is yours. Renee gave notice yesterday. As soon as Jim's out, you're the new dramaturg– turge. I meant to tell you last night–

HEIDI. *(pulling away)* I just wanted Renee's job! I didn't want Jim fired!

MIKE. Jim's is the only job open. Renee's has been eliminated.

HEIDI. Then I'll stay an intern. Hire Jim back.

MIKE. *(crossing down)* I can't. I have a notebook documenting his incompetence.

HEIDI. I didn't mean for it to be taken that way.

MIKE. Then why did you write it? Can you really be so naïve, after all the times I talked about having things in writing? I wasn't saying let's redecorate the office, I was giving you a license to kill. *(sitting on edge of desk)* And you not only accepted that responsibility, you dragged his corpse behind your chariot for the whole city to see.

HEIDI. *(crossing down left)* My ambition got the better of me.

MIKE. I know. That's what I first admired about you.

HEIDI. Why didn't you tell me you were firing Jim?

MIKE. I was going to.

HEIDI. *(crossing to MIKE)* When? Afterwards? When I was cradled in your arms, completely in your power? You might have a sexual harassment lawsuit on your hands.

MIKE. *(crossing down right)* Okay. At no point did I make a quid pro quo exchange of Jim's job for sex. At no point did I make a physical advance that was unwanted or unreciprocated. The dinner we had was a business meeting originated by you. At no point did I ever make lewd comments, jokes, or references to or about you or any other woman in this theater that could create a hostile environment. No one is more careful than me about the appearance of impropriety. Ask anyone. Like a cable channel, I am all business, all the time. If anyone in this office is being harassed right now, it is me.

HEIDI. You've got to be–!

MIKE. You're threatening to sue me over a sexual liaison to influence my decision on Jim's job. Last I heard, that's textbook extortion. If you'd be so kind as to write that threat down and sign it, I'd be more than happy to report it to the local police. ...No? Then let's move on.

(**HEIDI** *crosses up center.* **MIKE** *crosses to exit.*)

HEIDI. What if I refuse to take the job?

MIKE. You're not gonna refuse the job.

HEIDI. How do you know?

(**HEIDI** *sits on desk edge.*)

MIKE. Then don't take it. You're lucky it's still on the table. You think you're the only one looking for this kind of work? If I ever need a dramaturg, I just go to New Haven, stand on the corner of York Street and toss a brick. Face it. You're on the losing end of this no matter where you turn. If you want to quit, fine. Write me a note. I've already wasted enough energy on this. Dramaturgy is the least important creative role in non-profit theater. Non-profit theater is the least important element of show business. And show business is the least important necessity for life on earth. That's how small your concerns are.

HEIDI. (*crossing to* **MIKE**) Your concerns are just as small as mine.

MIKE. Mine are making money.

(**MIKE** *exits.* **HEIDI** *is furious. She sits behind her desk. She picks up the Hrosvitha book and looks at the cover. She brings the book to her nose and inhales with pleasure.* **TINA** *enters.*)

TINA. So you're back to air freshener.

(**TINA** *crosses up right.*)

HEIDI. Oh, hey. I heard about the show going to New York.

TINA. Did I leave my glasses in here last night?

HEIDI. You're welcome to look. ...I heard you got a standing ovation.

TINA. (*looking around*) You didn't see it?

HEIDI. Box office. I wanted to talk to you about it last night, but…

(**HEIDI** *trails off, getting an idea.*)

TINA. Ha! Found them.

(**TINA** *starts to exit with her glasses.* **HEIDI** *stands.*)

HEIDI. Have you got a minute?

TINA. I don't want to miss my train.

HEIDI. I need to talk to you. To ask a favor.

TINA. *(leaning against the wall)* Professional or personal?

HEIDI. Kind of both.

TINA. I might be able to spare a minute.

(**TINA** *crosses to* **JIM***'s chair.*)

HEIDI. It's about Mike Braschi. He's handling the transfer?

TINA. They'll need him.

HEIDI. *(crossing down right)* Would it be possible… for you to insist that Mike not be involved at all?

(**TINA** *smiles at the cruelty of the notion.*)

TINA. Why?

HEIDI. Because I don't like him.

TINA. And you want me to risk everybody's money for that?

HEIDI. Well, there's more to it–

TINA. I mean, I don't like him either, but–

HEIDI Okay. Last night Mike fired Jim.

TINA. And he didn't promote you?

HEIDI. *(crossing down left)* He did promote me, but–

TINA. Then why are you upset?

HEIDI. I'm upset because Jim got screwed over and Mike used me.

TINA. It's still not enough to make me risk a flop.

HEIDI. But what about Jim? He's your dramaturg.

TINA. I've got a new dramaturg.

HEIDI. Who?

TINA. You.

HEIDI. *(crossing below her desk)* …Jim's a better dramaturg than I am.

TINA. He used to be. But he's not as on-the-ball as you. I go where success lies.

HEIDI I don't have anything to offer.

TINA. Sure you do.

HEIDI. What.

TINA. How does this sound? I'll do it. Okay? *(standing and crossing downstage)* I'll call up the producers soon as I get home and have Mike canned. *(sitting on JIM's desk)* …All you have to do–is come *with* me.

HEIDI. Come with you? What does that mean?

TINA. It means 'turg the transfer. Come with me to New York. We'll work side by side.

HEIDI. Mike won't allow that.

TINA. But Janet will, if I talk to her.

HEIDI. *(sitting beside TINA)* What happens when the show closes?

TINA. We'll discuss it when it occurs. I'm sure we can come to some arrangement.

(TINA moves an errant lock of HEIDI's hair. HEIDI stands.)

HEIDI. Whoa! Uh–

(HEIDI crosses down left)

TINA. Is that so unexpected?

HEIDI. Um, well, yeah.

TINA. Come on. Who are you kidding? You've been trying to get my attention since you first saw me. You've got it now.

HEIDI. That's not the kind of attention I was looking for.

TINA. Women don't interest you?

HEIDI. No, I've been to college.

(TINA stands and crosses up center.)

–It's just: I've always seen our relationship as exclusively professional, not sexual.

TINA. *(leaning against the wall)* One will get you the other.

HEIDI. I'm flattered, really. But that's not how I work.

TINA. Isn't it? I'm pretty sure it was you they were talking about last night.

HEIDI. Wait–Talking? Last night?

TINA. This morning too, as I was coming in. The rumors are everywhere.

HEIDI. About me?

TINA. And Mike. Having dinner together, leaving the party–

HEIDI. Oh my God.

TINA. *(crossing to* **JIM**'s *chair)* And now you've got Jim's job.

HEIDI. *(stepping in)* Is that what they're saying? That I–That's not the way it happened! Jim's job was the furthest thing from my mind!

TINA. You made no secret of your ambition.

HEIDI. But I don't sleep with the boss to get ahead! That's not who I am!

TINA. That's the type Mike usually goes for.

HEIDI. Is *he* saying this? Is he the one who–?

TINA. He's not denying it. *Everyone's* saying it. They saw you leave together. At the party–

HEIDI. *(moving down left)* Oh my God. Oh my God! SHIT!!! How can I ever–? FUCK! *(crossing to* **TINA***)* What about Janet?

TINA. I'm sure she's accustomed to Mike promoting his–

HEIDI. Fuck that. Has Janet heard the rumors? Does she think I'm Mike's slut? I'll never go anywhere! *(crossing down right)* –Okay, what can I do. There's gotta be something I can–FUCK!!!

TINA. It's not the end of the world.

HEIDI. It is to *my* world! I'll never be able to set foot outside that door again! –I'm ruined.

(**HEIDI** *sits on* **JIM**'s *desk. Though there may be tears in her eyes, she does not cry.)*

TINA. *(crossing down left)* There is a way out. …Are you listening? There's a way forward. …Heidi.

(**HEIDI** *looks up at* **TINA**.)

You don't have to face them ever again.

(**TINA** *crosses down right*)

If you're looking to get out of here, I'm offering a way. —Come with me to New York. Don't be afraid to grab that next level. I'm offering everything you ever wanted.

HEIDI. In exchange for my soul.

TINA. I'm an artist, I have no soul.

HEIDI. But I do.

TINA. I find it adorable that you think so. —Come with me, and all of this will disappear. Once you're past the threshold of success, no one cares what compromises you made to get through. Reputation is the topic of the envious and impolite.

(**TINA** *moves in. She touches* **HEIDI**'s *chin*.)

Do you want to succeed?

(**TINA** *kisses* **HEIDI** *gently*.)

I'll take that as a yes.

(**TINA** *exits.* **HEIDI** *begins to cry. She moves to her chair and holds the book close to her chest.* **JIM** *enters, carrying a cup of coffee.* **HEIDI** *runs into the conference chamber to hide her emotions.*)

JIM. Ruining my life wasn't enough for you, hmm? You had to go and ruin yours too.

HEIDI. (*off*) Leave me alone.

JIM. (*crossing up center*) You know what Mike's saying about you at the coffee machine?

HEIDI. (*off*) Go away!

JIM. (*crossing up right*) No, you come out here. We both screwed up. I think we can face each other honestly and without shame. *Well…* Come on out. At least we can share a moment of mutual schadenfreude, delighting in each other's falls.

(**HEIDI** *comes to the doorway.* **JIM** *moves left.*)

HEIDI. I don't delight in your fall.

JIM. Well, I don't delight in yours either.

HEIDI. *(moving in)* …Really?

JIM. –Maybe a little.

(**HEIDI** *smiles grimly in spite of herself.*)

HEIDI. Maybe a lot.

JIM. Here. *(putting the coffee cup on her desk)* Peace offering. …Go on.

HEIDI. Is it poisoned?

JIM. No.

HEIDI. *(crossing to her desk)* Too bad. Death is an effective cure for bad choices.

JIM You blew it. No question. But if I were in your situation, just starting out, I might have made the same choices.

HEIDI. *(sitting at her desk)* I didn't do it knowingly.

JIM. *(crossing up right)* I did. In Boston. Many years ago. I was on running crew, reading scripts when I could, like you. Our literary associate had a thing for college boys on the crew, so I tried to get into his good graces by setting him up with a couple after every matinee. I'd be in charge of the office, playing lookout, while he was off doing his thing. One day Tina showed up, asked me where he was and I told her. The next day I had his job.

HEIDI. …Maybe I did do it knowingly. I don't know.

JIM. *(crossing to her)* Drink up.

(**JIM** *sips the coffee to prove it isn't poisoned.* **HEIDI** *takes a sip.*)

Turning to Hrosvitha for advice?

HEIDI. Remembering simpler times.

JIM. They're never simple while you're living them.

(**HEIDI** *smiles.*)

HEIDI. You need to challenge every sentence I utter, don't you?

JIM. Not every sentence. Eighty percent tops.

HEIDI. What am I going to do without you?

JIM. You're gonna find a way to clear your reputation and hang on to this job. You're only here as long as Mike wants you.

HEIDI. What should I do?

JIM. Get it in writing.

(**JIM** *begins to pack his things.*)

HEIDI. What about you? What are you gonna do?

(**JIM** *shrugs.* **HEIDI** *crosses below her desk.*)

Have you ever done any directing?

JIM. I don't need your pity.

HEIDI. Not in the future, in the past.

JIM. A little, here and there. Playwriting too.

HEIDI. *(leaning on desk)* Really?

JIM. *(collecting books from the book shelf)* All dramaturgs dabble. You could almost define a dramaturg as someone unable to find work as a director or playwright, who decides to make things more difficult for the ones who did find work.

HEIDI. *(smiling)* Kind of like Shaw's definition of a teacher.

JIM. *(crossing to* **HEIDI***)* I could never work as a director. I don't have enough friends. That's how directors get hired. They're the only theater people with friends.

(**JIM** *sits at his desk.*)

HEIDI. What about playwrights?

JIM. *(packing his pills)* Please! Playwrights don't have friends. Playwrights skulk in corners with leather patches on their sleeves, greeting each other with *Star Trek* salutes. I've never met a playwright who couldn't recite verbatim entire episodes of *Monty Python*. Pathetic, lonely, friendless people.

HEIDI. Actors don't have friends?

JIM. Not 'til they look in the mirror.

HEIDI. How about producers?

JIM. Only enemies to destroy.

HEIDI. Stage hands.

JIM. Only beverage buddies.

HEIDI. Designers?

JIM. In those clothes?

HEIDI. *(standing)* Dramaturgs.

JIM. Dramaturgs barely have jobs–!

> *(Their smiles and laughter fade to an awkward pause.* **JIM** *stands.)*

> …I better get home–to pack scripts.

> *(***JIM*** *exits.* **HEIDI** *dials the phone.)*

HEIDI. Janet! I know I shouldn't call you on your cell, but you got a minute? –Heidi Bishop.

> *(Blackout. Scene change audio begins.)*

Scene Change 6

(The elevator pitch)

PRODUCER. You've got til we reach my floor. Start talking.

SCREENWRITER. *(Irish accent)* A desolate field, with nothing but a dead tree and the sun beating down on a pair of figures.

PRODUCER. Nice. What are they doing?

SCREENWRITER. Waiting.

PRODUCER. For what?

SCREENWRITER. For a gent who never shows up.

PRODUCER. Pass. What else.

SCREENWRITER. Okay, there's a bloke in a wheelchair. He has an obsessive need to be in the center of the room and his parents are in trashcans.

PRODUCER. Is he a serial killer?

SCREENWRITER. No, he's a symbol of the author's unconscious, a character who is himself a creator.

PRODUCER. And what do they do?

SCREENWRITER. End.

PRODUCER. End??? They end??? I don't even know what that means. Pass.

SCREENWRITER. Okay, there's an old man listening to his diary and eating bananas–

PRODUCER. Pass.

SCREENWRITER. An old woman sinking in mud–!

PRODUCER. Pass!

SCREENWRITER. A disembodied mouth–!

(An elevator bell is heard, along with the door opening.)

PRODUCER. Look, buddy, this is my floor, okay? You had your shot. Here's five dollars. Take it.

SCREENWRITER. What for?

PRODUCER. Writing lessons.

(lights up on scene four)

Scene 4

(The next day. A human form sits behind Jim's desk, obscured by a large newspaper ostensibly being read. The phone rings. A hand appears from behind the newspaper, picks up the phone a half inch and immediately returns it to its cradle. Pause. The phone rings again. The hand silences it again. A third time the phone rings. **HEIDI**—*the form—sighs angrily, puts down the paper and silences the phone a third time. She waits for the next ring. It doesn't come. The Hrosvitha book is now on* **JIM**'s *desk.* **JIM** *enters, struggling with a large box filled with scripts. He crosses to the upstage left script pile.)*

JIM. Nineteen more to go.

HEIDI. You want me to help?

JIM. It's too much for you.

HEIDI. You always underestimate me.

JIM. *(putting the box atop the pile)* This is one of the small ones.

HEIDI. Where am I going to put it all?

JIM. You really want me to suggest where you should put them?

*(***JIM** *starts to exit, bumping into* **TINA** *again.)*

Excuse me, Dumpling.

TINA. Where are you going?

JIM. To get another box from my car. Congratulations, by the way.

TINA. I came to say good bye to you.

JIM. Well, you're going to have to wait. On my last day of work, I intend to see that you finally miss that fucking train.

*(***JIM** *exits.)*

HEIDI. Congratulations!

TINA. That's all anyone says to me anymore.

(The phone rings. **HEIDI** *lifts and replaces the receiver.)*

What's that for?

HEIDI. Mike.

TINA. *(crossing upstage left)* You don't have to worry about him ever again.

HEIDI. That's probably why he's calling.

> *(The phone rings.* **HEIDI** *lifts and replaces the receiver.* **TINA** *sits.)*

TINA. Does he know you're coming in his place yet?

HEIDI. I'm keeping that secret. Your show just opened here. It won't move to New York for awhile. In the meantime, I need to keep *this* job. –Have you seen the reviews?

TINA. I don't give a damn about that.

HEIDI. I wish I didn't care, but it's the first big show I ever worked on. I was worried about how the monologue might be received.

TINA. And?

HEIDI. No mention at all.

TINA. Good. That's good.

HEIDI. But it gets better. Listen to this: *(reading from the newspaper)* Okay, acting... Janet's direction... Here we go: "Hats must be lifted to Fike for not caving in to the more glossy and vapid elements of what passes for theater this season. She hits us early and often with the political and emotional invective that has character-ized her work for the last four decades. This play acts as a fine capstone, if not a fond farewell to one of the great writers of the previous century."

TINA. Does it really say that?

HEIDI. *(handing* **TINA** *the paper)* Right here.

> *(***TINA** *stands and crosses downstage right while reading the paper.)*

TINA. Would you look at that. He was right again.

HEIDI. Who.

TINA. Jim. The monologue needs to go.

HEIDI. But they loved it. They practically repeated all my arguments in favor of it.

TINA. *(crossing upstage right)* They said it was old fashioned. "Previous century," "fond farewell." These are horrible words.

*(*TINA* throws the paper in the trash.)*

HEIDI. They found it refreshing.

TINA. Refreshing means "contrary to what people want to see."

HEIDI. But it brings closure–

TINA. I don't want closure. *(working around down left)* I have too many more plays to write. Just because I'm almost sixty-five doesn't mean I have to retire. There's too much more to say, too many inner demons left to exorcise. Besides, it's just a tangential rant. If the monologue's really that good, I can put it in whatever play I want. I'll put it in my final play. The one that demands closure.

HEIDI. Well, there it is.

TINA. What.

HEIDI. The final nail in the coffin of my youth.

TINA. Oh, God. Get over yourself.

HEIDI. *(standing)* But everything I did was based on my faith in that monologue.

TINA. So what.

HEIDI. So…I can't work for you.

TINA. Whoa! Nobody bails on me.

HEIDI. You don't need me. You don't need any dramaturg. I'm just one small part of the vast theatrical organism. Imposed on it, like a virus.

TINA. Or a vaccine.

HEIDI. *(turning away)* What's the point? Nobody cares about the theater anyway.

TINA. Let's talk.

(The phone rings. TINA *barks into the receiver.)*

Stop calling!

(She hangs up. **TINA** *moves a chair below the desks and invites* **HEIDI** *to sit.)*

Listen. *(crossing upstage right)* Forty years ago, when I first started, ninety-nine percent of the American public had no idea what a dramaturg was. Today that number is down to ninety-eight percent. Depressing? For you, probably. *(crossing downstage right)* But not when you consider that most of the American public has no idea what a director does, or that no one can name ten living playwrights. It's just the nature of the beast. *(sitting on Jim's desk)* Theater means nothing anymore. It's the worst field trip you ever took in high school. It's the blow-off course you took in college for an A. We all know this. We don't come right out and say it to each other, but deep down we know it to be true.

HEIDI. Then why bother?

TINA. Maybe you shouldn't. People don't *choose* to work in the theater. They don't ponder what profession will result in a lifetime of rejection, no money, and even less recognition or advancement, and then actively pursue it. The choice is made for them. It's a calling, like being a priest but with a lot more sex. Come to think of it, that's an accurate analogy. The Catholic church is a lot like theater. Both deal with our place in society and the universe. Both concentrate their wealth and power in a single city–New York, Rome–while the outlying organizations are forced to scramble for donations. And both have seen declining attendance over the last hundred years. But they keep going. What I write is the gospel. The director is the priest, the actors are the altar servers.

HEIDI. What is the dramaturg?

TINA. Ah, that's the good one. The dramaturg is the prophet. You assist the gospel writer, you help the priest interpret the holy text, you write epistles expounding your faith. You are misunderstood. Ignored. And sometimes? You're martyred. –Prophets lead horrible

TINA. *(cont.)* lives. Nobody chooses to become a prophet. They choose *not* to become prophets. This is the choice you need to make.

(a pause)

HEIDI. You're bullshitting.

TINA. One hundred percent. –Everything is small if you consider it small. What makes something big is the amount of effort you put into it. ...You have become what Jim wanted you to become.

(TINA leans back on the desk. Her hand rests on the Hrosvitha book.)

HEIDI. What's that?

TINA. *(laughing)* Oh God, is he still foisting this book on people?

HEIDI. Who?

TINA. *(picking up the Hrosvitha book)* Jim. He's making you read that medieval crap he translated.

HEIDI. Hrosvitha? Jim did the translation?

TINA. *(crossing upstage right with book)* He did a bunch of them a few years ago. Who's the publisher? Yeah, that's his. He making you read it?

HEIDI. I picked it up on my own.

TINA. And he never said anything?

HEIDI. No.

(TINA laughs and shakes her head.)

TINA. I'm gonna miss my train.

(HEIDI regards the book in a different manner as MIKE enters angrily.)

MIKE. Why aren't you answering the phone?

HEIDI. I'd appreciate it if you'd knock.

MIKE. You're hanging up on me.

HEIDI. What?

MIKE. You're playing Jim's old game, hanging up the phone when it rings.

HEIDI. I didn't hear a ring.

TINA. *(placing the book back on the desk)* Is Jim still out there?

MIKE. Try the unemployment line.

TINA. I don't give a damn about that.

(**TINA** *exits.* **MIKE** *and* **HEIDI** *face off.*)

HEIDI. I was meeting with our playwright. Is that a problem?

(**HEIDI** *crosses to* **JIM**'s *desk and reaches for a cigarette of her own.*)

MIKE. There's no smoking.

HEIDI. *(failing to light it)* Really. That's very interesting.

MIKE. Cut it out. Right now. –The Niederberts. This morning. They don't want me involved in the transfer.

HEIDI. Oh, no. Did they give a reason?

MIKE. No, they didn't give me a fucking reason. Why don't *you* give me a reason?

HEIDI. Me? I'm just an insignificant dramaturg.

MIKE. I know you did this. I don't know how, or who you called, but I'm going to find out.

HEIDI. Does this mean you'll be sticking around here a little longer?

MIKE. Unlike you. You're fired! Get the fuck out!

HEIDI. Boy, I bet firing me would have felt good if you still had the power to do it. *(crossing to her bag beside her former desk)* But you see, I've got something in writing.

(**HEIDI** *pulls a memo from the bag. She hands it to* **MIKE.**)

From Janet, your boss. You'll be getting a copy of it this afternoon, probably. Anyway, because of the romantic, sexual relationship you and I share, Janet didn't think it a good idea that you oversee this department. So I don't answer to you anymore. I answer to her. In other words, you can't fire me. All you can do is stop fucking me.

(beat)

MIKE. Fuck!!!

*(**MIKE** storms out.)*

HEIDI. See you in New York!

*(**HEIDI** laughs. She stubs out her unlit cigarette at **JIM**'s desk. **JIM** enters with another huge box, placing it on Heidi's desk.)*

JIM. God, this is all I need. I'm gonna rupture something.

HEIDI. *(stepping closer)* Did Tina say "good-bye?"

JIM. I caught her outside.

HEIDI. Did she tell you about Big Mike Braschi?

JIM. How you're cutting him down to size? I give him two months before you take his place.

HEIDI. I don't intend to stick around that long.

JIM. Not even for revenge?

HEIDI. Well…

JIM. *(pointing to his desk)* I've a friend inside that drawer.

*(**HEIDI** peers into the drawer.)*

HEIDI. The bottle?

JIM. It will help me believe I can lift all those boxes.

*(**HEIDI** removes the scotch bottle and pours a shot for each of them. **JIM** proposes a toast.)*

To dramaturgy.

HEIDI. To prophecy.

JIM. What?

*(**HEIDI** clinks Jim's glass and drinks. He follows suit.)*

HEIDI. So what will you do now? Any plans?

JIM. *(crossing down right)* That's what Tina wanted to see me about. She asked me to transfer with the show to New York.

HEIDI. She… what?

JIM. As dramaturg.

HEIDI. You???

JIM. The producers had someone else in mind, but she needed to go where success lies.

(**JIM** *crosses upstage right.* **HEIDI** *stares left, shocked.*)

HEIDI. Well… Jim, that's–that's fantastic. I'm very, very happy for you.

JIM. Well, it will keep me going until the show closes.

HEIDI. *(turning to him)* Then what?

JIM. Who knows? She mentioned something about writing a recommendation.

HEIDI. To do what?

JIM. *(crossing to Heidi's desk)* To teach college.

HEIDI. *(crossing downstage right)* Oh no!

JIM. Yes, I intend to flood the market with even more young turgs. Training each of them to take your place.

HEIDI. Abandon all hope, ye who intern here.

JIM. But that is later. First I need to make it through today.

(**JIM** *starts to exit.*)

HEIDI. Before I forget. *(crossing to* **JIM***'s desk)* I need you to do something.

JIM. What.

HEIDI. Don't worry. Very small. But it will mean a lot to me.

(She hands him the Hrosvitha book and a pen.)

Could you sign my copy?

JIM. Who told you–?

HEIDI. Blame it on Beckett. Heidi is E, I.

JIM. You don't want me to–

HEIDI. I do. …It will mean a lot to me.

(**JIM** *sits on the edge of one of the desks and writes something in the book. He closes it and hands it back to her.*)

Thank you.

JIM. Let's move boxes.

(They start to exit. The phone rings.)

JIM. Let it ring.

*(**JIM** exits. **HEIDI** can't let it ring. She sits at Jim's desk and answers the phone.)*

HEIDI. Literary. …mm-hmm. …Don't be silly, I love talking to all of our playwrights. *(genuinely)* Love it, love it, love it.

*(**HEIDI** reads what Jim wrote in the Hrosvitha book and chuckles in spite of herself.)*

What was the title again? Oh, that's the one I just gave to Janet for the reading series! You made it past the first hurdle…

*(**HEIDI** sits back as the curtain descends.)*

PROPERTIES LIST

Top of Show

Desk lamp turned off

Trash has 2 bags, tucked to sides

Scripts on desk

5 Scripts on chair

Scripts on Heidi desk

Tina poster askew

4 prescription bottles half full in upper right drawer

Post it notes in front of sharpener

Folder with lighter on desk

Jim's Jacket on chair

Cigarettes in jacket pocket

Jim's attaché in front of desk

Jim's copy of Tina's script in bottom left drawer

Jim's Yellow Pad w/ pages of notes in bottom left drawer

Jim's pen attached to pad

Clean copy of Tina's script in bottom left drawer

Script reports in folders in bottom left drawer

Script reports in folder in bottom right drawer

Paper towels in top left drawer

Clicky pens in center drawer

Yellow Pad in center drawer

The notebook on shelf

2 Empty cups upright/covered on DS corner of desk

1 Empty cup upright/covered on US corner of desk

2 Empty cups in front of desk

Empty cup by conference door

Empty cup on Heidi desk

Empty cup under Heidi desk

Empty cup on USL scripts

Cup with three gulps of coffee (1.1) middle left drawer

Cup with inch of coffee (1.1) DSR script stack

Lidless Cup (1.3) on USR top shelf

"Hairdresser" script top of DSR script stack

"Polyphemus" script second on DSR script stack

Jim's pen on Desk

Small notepads in top three drawers

Act II Presets

Scotch bottle with cap off

Scotch box

3 Scripts DS corner of desk

Tina's glasses

Heidi's bag

Memo in Heidi's bag

Desk lamp turned on

Props Table Act I

Wallet with dollars

Heidi's bag

　"Hrosvitha" in Heidi's bag

　Money purse in Heidi's bag

Tina's bag

　Glasses in Tina's bag

　Sun glasses in Tina's bag

　Folder with changes in Tina's bag

Coffee cup with coffee 1.2 Tina

Coffee cup with coffee 1.2 Heidi

"Hairdresser" script report

Script Heidi's working on with pen

Flower for desk

Hartford Courant

Air Freshener

Mail

5 page handwritten script

Props Table Act II

Scotch glass with iced tea

Scotch glass

Pink slip envelope

Party glass with water

Party glass with water

Cup with coffee 2.3 Jim

Newspaper

Large box of scripts

Large box of scripts

COSTUME PLOT

Heidi

Act 1/Sc 1 - beige skirt, cream sweater, scarf, pumps

Act 1/Sc 2 - beige pants, salmon sweater, flats, scarf

Act 1/Sc 3 - beige pants, blue blouse, flats,

Act 1/Sc 4 - beige pants, purple cardigan sweater, flats

Act 2/Sc 2 - rust colored cocktail dress, pumps

Act 2/Sc 3 - rust colored cocktail dress, pumps

Act 2/Sc 4 - Heidi, grey dress, black flats

Jim

Act 1/Sc 1 - Brown corduroy pants, button down shirt, tie, digital watch, shoes, belt

Act 1/Sc 2 - Brown corduroy pants, button down shirt, tie, sweater vest, digital watch, shoes, belt

Act 1/Sc 3 - Brown corduroy pants, button down shirt, tie, digital watch, shoes, belt

Act 1/Sc 4 - Brown corduroy pants, button down shirt, tie, digital watch, shoes, belt

Act 2/Sc 1 - Brown corduroy suit, silk scarf, button down shirt, tie, digital watch, shoes, belt

Act 2/Sc 2 - Brown corduroy suit, silk scarf, button down shirt, tie, digital watch, shoes, belt

Act 2/Sc 3 - Brown corduroy suit, silk scarf, button down shirt, tie, digital watch, shoes, belt

Act 2/Sc 4 - Brown corduroy pants, navy blue polo, shoes, digital watch

Mike

Act 1/Sc 2 - beige suit, maroon button down, tie, cordovan shoes, cordovan belt

Act 1/Sc 3 - khaki pants, button down shirt, red tie, blue sports coat, cordovan belt, cordovan shoes

Act 1/Sc 4 - beige suit, button down, tie, cordovan shoes, cordovan belt

Act 2/Sc 1 - suit #2, button down, tie, suspenders, black shoes

Act 2/Sc 2 - suit #2, button down, tie, suspenders, black shoes

Act 2/Sc 3 - beige suit, button down, tie, cordovan shoes, cordovan belt

Act 2/Sc 4 - khaki pants, button down shirt, red tie, cordovan belt, cordovan shoes

Tina

Act 1/Sc 2 - blouse, cream pants, tank top, accessories

Act 1/Sc 3 - black cardigan, black pants, grey tank top, accessories

Act 2/Sc 1 - black pants, black cardigan, lilac tank top, black mules, accessories

Act 2/Sc 3 - black tunic, brown pants, accessories

Act 2/Sc 4 - blouse, cream pants, tank top, accessories

BLAME IT ON BECKETT GROUND PLAN

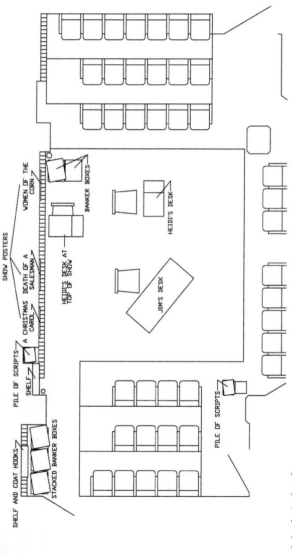

Set design by Andrew Lu

Lightning Source UK Ltd.
Milton Keynes UK
UKHW02f2354170118
316332UK00006B/205/P